Distributed Computing with Go

Practical concurrency and parallelism for Go applications

V.N. Nikhil Anurag

BIRMINGHAM - MUMBAI

Distributed Computing with Go

Commissioning Editor: Dominic Shakeshaft
Acquisition Editor: Frank Pohlmann
Project Editor: Radhika Atitkar
Content Development Editor: Monika Sangwan
Technical Editor: Nidhisha Shetty
Copy Editor: Tom Jacob
Proofreader: Safis Editing
Indexer: Rekha Nair
Graphics: Tom Scaria
Production Coordinator: Nilesh Mohite

First published: February 2018

Production reference: 1270218

Published by Packt Publishing Ltd.
Livery Place
35 Livery Street
Birmingham
B3 2PB, UK.

ISBN 978-1-78712-538-4

www.packtpub.com

`mapt.io`

Mapt is an online digital library that gives you full access to over 5,000 books and videos, as well as industry leading tools to help you plan your personal development and advance your career. For more information, please visit our website.

Why subscribe?

- Spend less time learning and more time coding with practical eBooks and Videos from over 4,000 industry professionals

- Improve your learning with Skill Plans built especially for you

- Get a free eBook or video every month

- Mapt is fully searchable

- Copy and paste, print, and bookmark content

PacktPub.com

Did you know that Packt offers eBook versions of every book published, with PDF and ePub files available? You can upgrade to the eBook version at `www.PacktPub.com` and as a print book customer, you are entitled to a discount on the eBook copy. Get in touch with us at `service@packtpub.com` for more details.

At `www.PacktPub.com`, you can also read a collection of free technical articles, sign up for a range of free newsletters, and receive exclusive discounts and offers on Packt books and eBooks.

Contributors

About the author

V.N. Nikhil Anurag is a Go developer currently working in Berlin. He speaks at conferences about how to use Go in domains such as Concurrency, file systems, and distributed systems. He is also trying to bridge the gap between the rich literature on concurrency and the practice of programming goroutines and channels. He did his Bachelor's in Electronics and Instrumentation Engineering from JNTU, India and Master of Science in Control System from University of Sheffield, UK.

About the reviewers

Pankaj Khairnar is a cofounder and CTO at Qwentic (A Golang specialized development company). He loves programming, and for the last 10 years, he has been developing highly scalable and distributed enterprise applications using various technologies.

I would like to thank my wife and friends for their support.

Jinzhu Zhang is a veteran coder, creator/contributor of many open source projects, such as GORM. He is on Github at github.com/jinzhu.

Packt is searching for authors like you

If you're interested in becoming an author for Packt, please visit authors.packtpub.com and apply today. We have worked with thousands of developers and tech professionals, just like you, to help them share their insight with the global tech community. You can make a general application, apply for a specific hot topic that we are recruiting an author for, or submit your own idea.

Table of Contents

Preface

The Go programming language was developed at Google to solve the problems they faced while developing software for their infrastructure. They needed a language that was statically typed without slowing down the developer, would compile and execute instantaneously, take advantage of multicore processors, and make working across distributed systems, effortless.

The mission of **Distributed computing with Go** is to make reasoning about concurrency and parallelism, effortless and provide the reader with the confidence to design and implement such programs in Go. We will start by digging into the core concepts behind goroutines and channels, the two fundamental concepts in Go around which the language is built. Next, we will design and build a distributed search engine using Go and Go's standard library.

Who this book is for

This book is for developers who are familiar with the Golang syntax and have a good idea of how basic Go development works. It would be advantageous if you have been through a web application product cycle, although it's not necessary.

What this book covers

Chapter 1, *Developer Environment for Go*, covers a list of topics and concepts required to start working with Go and rest of the book. Some of these topics include Docker and testing in Go.

Chapter 2, *Understanding Goroutines*, introduces the topic of concurrency and parallelism and then dives deep into the implementation details of goroutines, Go's runtime scheduler, and many more.

Chapter 3, *Channels and Messages*, begins by explaining the complexity of controlling parallelism before introducing strategies to control parallelism, using different types of channels.

Chapter 4, *The RESTful Web*, provides all the context and knowledge required to start designing and building REST APIs in Go. We will also discuss the interaction with a REST API server using different available approaches.

Chapter 5, *Introducing Goophr*, opens the discussion on what is meant by a distributed search engine, using OpenAPI specification to describe REST APIs and describing the responsibilities of the components of a search engine, using OpenAPI. Finally, we'll describe the project structure.

Chapter 6, *Goophr Concierge*, dives deep into the first component of Goophr by describing in detail how the component is supposed to work. These concepts are further driven home with the help of architectural and logical flow diagrams. Finally, we'll look at how to implement and test the component.

Chapter 7, *Goophr Librarian*, is a detailed look at the component that is responsible for maintaining the index for the search terms. We also look at how to search for given terms and how to order our search results and many more. Finally, we'll look at how to implement and test the component.

Chapter 8, *Deploying Goophr*, brings together everything we have implemented in the previous three chapters and start the application on the local system. We will then test our design by adding a few documents and searching against them via the REST API.

Chapter 9, *Foundations of Web Scale Architecture*, is an introduction to the vast and complex topic on how to design and scale a system to meet with the demands at web scale. We will start with a single instance of a monolith running on a single server and scale it up to span across multiple region, have redundancy safeguards to ensure that the service is never down and many more.

To get the most out of this book

- The material in the book is designed to enable a hands-on approach. Throughout the book, a conscious effort has been made to provide all the relevant information to the reader beforehand so that, if the reader chooses, they can try to solve the problem on their own and then refer to the solution provided in the book.
- The code in the book does not have any Go dependencies beyond the standard library. This is done in order to ensure that the code examples provided in the book never change, and this also allows us to explore the standard library.

- The source code in the book should be placed at `$GOPATH/src/distributed-go`. The source code for examples given will be located inside the `$GOPATH/src/distributed-go/chapterX` folder, where X stands for the chapter number.
- Download and install Go from `https://golang.org/` and Docker from `https://www.docker.com/community-edition` website

Download the example code files

You can download the example code files for this book from your account at `http://www.packtpub.com`. If you purchased this book elsewhere, you can visit `http://www.packtpub.com/support` and register to have the files emailed directly to you.

You can download the code files by following these steps:

1. Log in or register at `http://www.packtpub.com`.
2. Select the **SUPPORT** tab.
3. Click on **Code Downloads & Errata**.
4. Enter the name of the book in the **Search** box and follow the on-screen instructions.

Once the file is downloaded, please make sure that you unzip or extract the folder using the latest version of:

- WinRAR / 7-Zip for Windows
- Zipeg / iZip / UnRarX for Mac
- 7-Zip / PeaZip for Linux

The code bundle for the book is also hosted on GitHub at `https://github.com/PacktPublishing/Distributed-Computing-with-Go`. In case there's an update to the code, it will be updated on the existing GitHub repository.

We also have other code bundles from our rich catalog of books and videos available at `https://github.com/PacktPublishing/`. Check them out!

Download the color images

We also provide a PDF file that has color images of the screenshots/diagrams used in this book. You can download it here:
https://www.packtpub.com/sites/default/files/downloads/DistributedComputingwith Go_ColorImages.pdf.

Conventions used

There are a number of text conventions used throughout this book.

CodeInText: Indicates code words in text, database table names, folder names, filenames, file extensions, pathnames, dummy URLs, user input, and Twitter handles. For example, "Mount the downloaded WebStorm-10*.dmg disk image file as another disk in your system."

A block of code is set as follows:

```
[default]
exten => s,1,Dial(Zap/1|30)
exten => s,2,Voicemail(u100)
exten => s,102,Voicemail(b100)
exten => i,1,Voicemail(s0)
```

When we wish to draw your attention to a particular part of a code block, the relevant lines or items are set in bold:

```
[default]
exten => s,1,Dial(Zap/1|30)
exten => s,2,Voicemail(u100)
exten => s,102,Voicemail(b100)
exten => i,1,Voicemail(s0)
```

Any command-line input or output is written as follows:

```
# cp /usr/src/asterisk-addons/configs/cdr_mysql.conf.sample
    /etc/asterisk/cdr_mysql.conf
```

Bold: Indicates a new term, an important word, or words that you see on the screen, for example, in menus or dialog boxes, also appear in the text like this. For example, "Select **System info** from the **Administration** panel."

Warnings or important notes appear like this.

 Tips and tricks appear like this.

Get in touch

Feedback from our readers is always welcome.

General feedback: Email `feedback@packtpub.com`, and mention the book's title in the subject of your message. If you have questions about any aspect of this book, please email us at `questions@packtpub.com`.

Errata: Although we have taken every care to ensure the accuracy of our content, mistakes do happen. If you have found a mistake in this book we would be grateful if you would report this to us. Please visit, `http://www.packtpub.com/submit-errata`, selecting your book, clicking on the **Errata Submission Form** link, and entering the details.

Piracy: If you come across any illegal copies of our works in any form on the internet, we would be grateful if you would provide us with the location address or website name. Please contact us at `copyright@packtpub.com` with a link to the material.

If you are interested in becoming an author: If there is a topic that you have expertise in and you are interested in either writing or contributing to a book, please visit `http://authors.packtpub.com`.

Reviews

Please leave a review. Once you have read and used this book, why not leave a review on the site that you purchased it from? Potential readers can then see and use your unbiased opinion to make purchase decisions, we at Packt can understand what you think about our products, and our authors can see your feedback on their book. Thank you!

For more information about Packt, please visit `packtpub.com`.

1

Developer Environment for Go

Go is a modern programming language built for the 21st century application development. Hardware and technology have advanced significantly over the past decade, and most of the other languages do not take advantage of these technical advancements. As we shall see throughout the book, Go allows us to build network applications that take advantage of concurrency and parallelism made available with multicore systems.

In this chapter, we will look at some of the topics required to work through rest of the book, such as:

- Go configuration—GOROOT, GOPATH, and so on.
- Go package management
- Project structure used throughout the book
- Container technology and how to use Docker
- Writing tests in Go

GOROOT

In order to run or build a Go project, we need to have access to the Go binary and its libraries. A typical installation of Go (instructions can be found at https://golang.org/dl/) on Unix-based systems will place the Go binary at /usr/bin/go. However, it is possible to install Go on a different path. In that case, we need to set the GOROOT environment variable to point to our Go installation path and also append it to our PATH environment variable.

GOPATH

Programmers tend to work on many projects and it is good practice to have the source code separate from nonprogramming-related files. It is a common practice to have the source code in a separate location or workspace. Every programming language has its own conventions on how the language-related projects should be set up and Go is no exception to this.

GOPATH is the most important environment variable the developer has to set. It tells the Go compiler where to find the source code for the project and its dependencies. There are conventions within the GOPATH that need to be followed, and they have to deal with folder hierarchies.

src/

This is the directory that will contain the source code of our projects and their dependencies. In general, we want our source code to have version control and be hosted on the cloud. It would also be great if we or anyone else could easily use our project. This requires a little extra setup on our part.

Let's imagine that our project is hosted at http://git-server.com/user-name/my-go-project. We want to clone and build this project on our local system. To make it properly work, we need to clone it to $GOPATH/src/git-server.com/user-name/my-go-project. When we build a Go project with dependencies for the first time, we will see that the src/ folder has many directories and subdirectories that contain the dependencies of our project.

pkg/

Go is a compiled programming language; we have the source code and code for the dependencies that we want to use in our project. In general, every time we build a binary, the compiler has to read the source code of our project and dependencies and then compile it to machine code. Compiling unchanged dependencies every time we compile our main program would lead to a very slow build process. This is the reason that **object files** exist; they allow us to compile dependencies into reusable machine code that can be readily included in our Go binary.

These object files are stored in $GOPATH/pkg; they follow a directory structure similar to that of src/, except that they are within a subdirectory. These directories tend to follow the naming pattern of <OS>_<CPU-Architecture>, because we can build executable binaries for multiple systems:

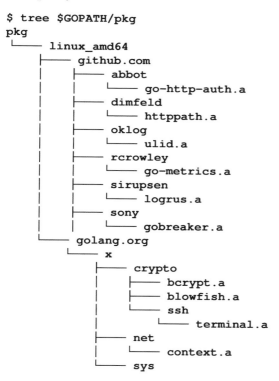

```
$ tree $GOPATH/pkg
pkg
└── linux_amd64
    ├── github.com
    │   ├── abbot
    │   │   └── go-http-auth.a
    │   ├── dimfeld
    │   │   └── httppath.a
    │   ├── oklog
    │   │   └── ulid.a
    │   ├── rcrowley
    │   │   └── go-metrics.a
    │   ├── sirupsen
    │   │   └── logrus.a
    │   ├── sony
    │   │   └── gobreaker.a
    └── golang.org
        └── x
            ├── crypto
            │   ├── bcrypt.a
            │   ├── blowfish.a
            │   └── ssh
            │       └── terminal.a
            ├── net
            │   └── context.a
            └── sys
```

bin/

Go compiles and builds our projects into executable binaries and places them in this directory. Depending on the build specs, they might be executable on your current system or other systems. In order to use the binaries that are available in the bin/ directory, we need to set the corresponding GOBIN=$GOPATH/bin environment variable.

Package management

In the days of yore, all programs were written from scratch—every utility function and every library to run the code had to written by hand. Now a days, we don't want to deal with the low level details on a regular basis; it would be unimaginable to write all the required libraries and utilities from scratch. Go comes with a rich library, which will be enough for most of our needs. However, it is possible that we might need a few extra libraries or features not provided by the standard library. Such libraries should be available on the internet, and we can download and add them into our project to start using them.

In the previous section, *GOPATH*, we discussed how all our projects are saved into qualified paths of the `$GOPATH/src/git-server.com/user-name/my-go-project` form. This is true for any and all dependencies we might have. There are multiple ways to handle dependencies in Go. Let's look at some of them.

go get

The `go get` is the utility provided by the standard library for package management. We can install a new package/library by running the following command:

```
$ go get git-server.com/user-name/library-we-need
```

This will download and build the source code and then install it as a binary executable (if it can be used as a standalone executable). The `go get` utility also installs all the dependencies required by the dependency retrieved for our project.

The `go get` utility is a very simple tool. It will install the latest master commit on the Git repository. For simple projects, this might be enough. However, as projects start growing in size and complexity, keeping track of the version of dependency being used might become critical. Unfortunately, `go get` is not great for such projects, and we might want to look at other package management tools.

glide

The glide is one of the most widely used package management tool in Go community. It addresses the limitations of go get, but it needs to be installed manually by the developer. The following is a simple way to install and use glide:

```
$ curl https://glide.sh/get | sh
$ mkdir new-project && cd new-project
$ glide create
$ glide get github.com/last-ent/skelgor # A helper project to generate
project skeleton.
$ glide install # In case any dependencies or configuration were manually
added.
$ glide up # Update dependencies to latest versions of the package.
$ tree
.
├── glide.lock
├── glide.yaml
└── vendor
    └── github.com
        └── last-ent
            └── skelgor
                ├── LICENSE
                ├── main.go
                └── README.md
```

In case you do not wish to install glide via curl and sh, other options are available and described in better detail on the project page, available at https://github.com/masterminds/glide.

go dep

The go dep is a new dependency management tool being developed by the Go community. Right now, it requires Go 1.7 or newer to compile, and it is ready for production use. However, it is still undergoing changes and hasn't yet been merged into Go's standard library.

Structuring a project

A project might have more than just the source code for the project, for example, configuration files and project documentation. Depending upon preferences, the way the project is structured can drastically change. However, the most important thing to remember is that the entry point to the whole program is through the `main` function, which is implemented within `main.go` as a convention.

The application we will be building in this book, will have the following initial structure:

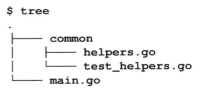

```
$ tree
.
├── common
│   ├── helpers.go
│   └── test_helpers.go
└── main.go
```

Working with book's code

The source code discussed throughout the book can be obtained in two ways:

- Using `go get -u github.com/last-ent/distributed-go`
- Downloading the code bundle from the website and extracting it to `$GOPATH/src/github.com/last-ent/distributed-go`

The code for complete book should now be available at `$GOPATH/src/github.com/last-ent/distributed-go` and the code specific for each chapter will be available in that particular chapter number's directory.

For example,

Code for Chapter 1 -> `$GOPATH/src/github.com/last-ent/distributed-go/chapter1`

Code for Chapter 2 -> `$GOPATH/src/github.com/last-ent/distributed-go/chapter2`

And so on.

Whenever we discuss code in any particular chapter, it is implied that we are in the respective chapter's folder.

Containers

Throughout the book, we will be writing Go programs that will be compiled to binaries and run directly on our system. However, in the latter chapters we will be using `docker-compose` to build and run multiple Go applications. These applications can run without any real problem on our local system; however, our ultimate goal is to be able to run these programs on servers and to be able to access them over the internet.

During the 1990s and early 2000s, the standard way to deploy applications to the internet was to get a server instance, copy the code or binary onto the instance, and then start the program. This worked great for a while, but soon complications began to arise. Here are a few of them:

- Code that worked on the developer's machine might not work on the server.
- Programs that ran perfectly on a server instance might fail upon applying the latest patch to the server's OS.
- For every new instance added as part of a service, various installation scripts had to be run so that we can bring the new instance to be on par with all the other instances. This can be a very slow process.
- Extra care had to be taken to ensure that the new instance and all the software versions installed on it are compatible with the APIs being used by our program.
- It was also important to ensure that all config files and important environment variables were copied to the new instance; otherwise, the application might fail with little or no clue.
- Usually the version of the program that ran on local system versus test system versus production system were all configured differently, and this meant that it was possible for our application to fail on one of the three types of systems. If such a situation occurred, we would end up having to spend extra time and effort trying to figure out whether the issue is specific to one particular instance, one particular system, and so on.

It would be great if we could avoid such a situation from arising, in a sensible manner. **Containers** try to solve this problem using OS-level virtualization. What does this mean?

All programs and applications are run in a section of memory known as **user space**. This allows the operating system to ensure that a program is not able to cause major hardware or software issues. This allows us to recover from any program crashes that might occur in the user space applications.

The real advantage of containers is that they allow us to run applications in isolated user spaces, and we can even customize the following attributes of user spaces:

- Connected devices such as network adapters and TTY
- CPU and RAM resources
- Files and folders accessible from host OS

However, how does this help us solve the problems we stated earlier? For that, let's take a deeper look at **Docker**.

Docker

Modern software development makes extensive use of containers for product development and product deployment to server instances. Docker is a container technology promoted by Docker, Inc (https://www.docker.com), and as of this writing, it is the most predominantly used container technology. The other major alternative is **rkt** developed by CoreOS (https://coreos.com/rkt), though in this book, we will only be looking at Docker.

Docker versus Virtual Machine (VM)

Looking at the description of Docker so far, we might wonder if it is yet another Virtual Machine. However, this is not the case, because a VM requires us to run a complete guest OS on top of our machine, or hypervisor, as well as all the required binaries. In the case of Docker, we use OS level virtualization, which allows us to run our containers in isolated user spaces.

The biggest advantage of a VM is that we can run different types of OSes on a system, for example, Windows, FreeBSD, and Linux. However, in the case of Docker, we can run any flavor of Linux, and the only limitation is that it has to be Linux:

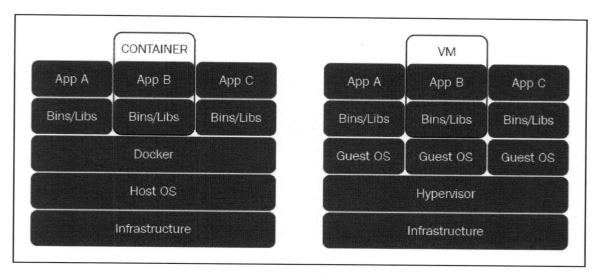

Docker container versus VM

The biggest advantage of Docker containers is that since it runs natively on Linux as a discrete process making it lightweight and unaware of all the capabilities of the host OS.

Understanding Docker

Before we start using Docker, let's take a brief look at how the Docker is meant to be used, how it is structured, and what are the major components of the complete system.

The following list and the accompanying image should help understand the architecture of Docker pipeline:

- **Dockerfile**: It consists of instructions on how to build an image that runs our program.
- **Docker client**: This is a command-line program used by the user to interact with Docker daemon.

- **Docker daemon**: This is the Daemon application that listens for commands to manage building or running containers and pushing containers to Docker registry. It is also responsible for configuring container networks, volumes, and so on.
- **Docker images**: Docker images contain all the steps necessary to build a container binary that can be executed on any Linux machine with Docker installed.
- **Docker registry**: The Docker registry is responsible for storing and retrieving the Docker images. We can use a public Docker registry or a private one. Docker Hub is used as the default Docker registry.
- **Docker Container**: The Docker container is different from the Container we have been discussing so far. A Docker container is a runnable instance of a Docker image. A Docker container can be created, started, stopped, and so on.
- **Docker API**: The Docker client we discussed earlier is a command-line interface to interact with Docker API. This means that the Docker daemon need not be running on the same machine as does the Docker client. The default setup that we will be using throughout the book talks to the Docker daemon on the local system using UNIX sockets or a network interface:

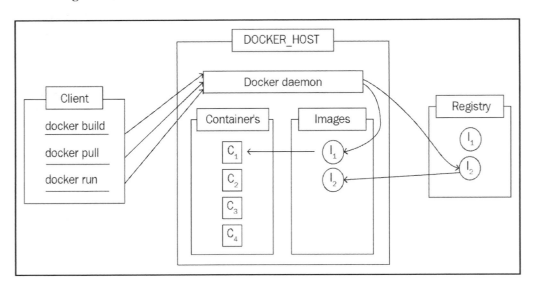

Docker architecture

Testing Docker setup

Let's ensure that our Docker setup works perfectly. For our purpose, Docker Community Edition should suffice (https://www.docker.com/community-edition). Once we have it installed, we will check if it works by running a few basic commands.

Let's start by checking what version we have installed:

```
$ docker --version
Docker version 17.12.0-ce, build c97c6d6
```

Let's try to dig deeper into details about our Docker installation:

```
$ docker info
Containers: 38
 Running: 0
 Paused: 0
 Stopped: 38
Images: 24
Server Version: 17.12.0-ce
```

 On Linux, when you try to run docker commands, you might get **Permission denied** error. In order to interact with Docker, you can either prefix the command with sudo or you can create a "docker" user group and add your user to this group. See link for more details https://docs.docker.com/install/linux/linux-postinstall/.

Let's try to run a Docker image. If you remember the discussion regarding the Docker registry, you know that we do not need to build a Docker image using Dockerfile, to run a Docker container. We can directly pull it from Docker Hub (the default Docker registry) and run the image as a container:

```
$ docker run docker/whalesay cowsay Welcome to GopherLand!

Unable to find image 'docker/whalesay:latest' locally
Trying to pull repository docker.io/docker/whalesay ...
sha256:178598e51a26abbc958b8a2e48825c90bc22e641de3d31e18aaf55f3258ba93b:
Pulling from docker.io/docker/whalesay
e190868d63f8: Pull complete
909cd34c6fd7: Pull complete
0b9bfabab7c1: Pull complete
a3ed95caeb02: Pull complete
00bf65475aba: Pull complete
c57b6bcc83e3: Pull complete
8978f6879e2f: Pull complete
8eed3712d2cf: Pull complete
```

```
Digest:
sha256:178598e51a26abbc958b8a2e48825c90bc22e641de3d31e18aaf55f3258ba93b
Status: Downloaded newer image for docker.io/docker/whalesay:latest
```

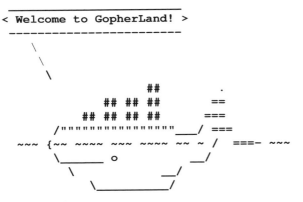

```
< Welcome to GopherLand! >
 -----------------------
    \
     \
      \
                    ##         .
              ## ## ##        ==
           ## ## ## ##       ===
       /"""""""""""""""""___/ ===
  ~~~ {~~ ~~~~ ~~~ ~~~~ ~~ ~ /  ===- ~~~
       _____ o          __/
        \    \        __/
         _____/
```

The preceding command could also have been executed, as shown here though, merely using `docker run ...`, which is more convenient:

```
$ docker pull  docker/whalesay & docker run docker/whalesay cowsay Welcome
to GopherLand!
```

Once we have a long set of built images, we can list them all and similarly for Docker containers:

```
$ docker images
REPOSITORY                      TAG            IMAGE ID
CREATED                 SIZE
docker.io/docker/whalesay    latest           6b362a9f73eb    2 years ago
247 MB
$ docker container ls --all
CONTAINER ID            IMAGE              COMMAND                 CREATED
STATUS                  PORTS              NAMES
a1b1efb42130            docker/whalesay    "cowsay Welcome to..."  5 minutes
ago         Exited (0) 5 minutes ago
frosty_varahamihira
```

Finally, it is important to note that as we keep using docker to build and run images and containers, we will start creating a backlog of "dangling" images, which we might not really use again. However, they will end up eating storage space. In order to get rid of such "dangling" images, we can use the following command:

```
$ docker rmi --force 'docker images -q -f dangling=true'
# list of hashes for all deleted images.
```

Dockerfile

Now that we have the basics of Docker under our belt, let's look at the `Dockerfile` file we will be using as a template in this book.

Next, let's look at an example:

```
FROM golang:1.10
# The base image we want to use to build our docker image from.
# Since this image is specialized for golang it will have GOPATH = /go

ADD . /go/src/hello
# We copy files & folders from our system onto the docker image

RUN go install hello
# Next we can create an executable binary for our project with the command,
'go install' ENV NAME Bob
# Environment variable NAME will be picked up by the program 'hello'
and printed to console.ENTRYPOINT /go/bin/hello
# Command to execute when we start the container

# EXPOSE 9000
# Generally used for network applications. Allows us to connect to the
application running inside the container from host system's localhost.
```

main.go

Let's create a bare minimum Go program so that we can use it in the Docker image. It will take the NAME environmental variable and print <NAME> is your uncle. and then quit:

```
package main

import (
    "fmt"
    "os"
)

func main() {
    fmt.Println(os.Getenv("NAME") + " is your uncle.")
}
```

Now that we have all the code in place, let's build the Docker image using the
`Dockerfile` file:

```
$ cd docker
$ tree
.
├── Dockerfile
└── main.go"
0 directories, 2 files

$ # -t tag lets us name our docker images so that we can easily refer to
them

$ docker build . -t hello-uncle
Sending build context to Docker daemon 3.072 kB
Step 1/5 : FROM golang:1.9.1
 ---> 99e596fc807e
Step 2/5 : ADD . /go/src/hello
 ---> Using cache
 ---> 64d080d7eb39
Step 3/5 : RUN go install hello
 ---> Using cache
 ---> 13bd4a1f2a60
Step 4/5 : ENV NAME Bob
 ---> Using cache
 ---> cc432fe8ffb4
Step 5/5 : ENTRYPOINT /go/bin/hello
 ---> Using cache
 ---> e0bbfb1fe52b
Successfully built e0bbfb1fe52b

$ # Let's now try to run the docker image.
$ docker run hello-uncle
Bob is your uncle.

$ # We can also change the environment variables on the fly.
$ docker run -e NAME=Sam hello-uncle
Sam is your uncle.
```

Testing in Go

Testing is an important part of programming, whether it is in Go or in any other language.
Go has a straightforward approach to writing tests, and in this section, we will look at some
important tools to help with testing.

There are certain rules and conventions we need to follow to test our code. They can be listed as follows:

- Source files and associated test files are placed in the same package/folder
- The name of the test file for any given source file is `<source-file-name>_test.go`
- Test functions need to have the "Test" prefix, and the next character in the function name should be capitalized

In the remainder of this section, we will look at three files and their associated tests:

- `variadic.go` and `variadic_test.go`
- `addInt.go` and `addInt_test.go`
- `nil_test.go` (there isn't any source file for these tests)

Along the way, we will introduce any further concepts we might use.

variadic.go

In order to understand the first set of tests, we need to understand what a variadic function is and how Go handles it. Let's start with the definition:

Variadic function is a function that can accept any number of arguments during function call.

Given that Go is a statically typed language, the only limitation imposed by the type system on a variadic function is that the indefinite number of arguments passed to it should be of the same data type. However, this does not limit us from passing other variable types. The arguments are received by the function as a slice of elements if arguments are passed, else `nil`, when none are passed.

Let's look at the code to get a better idea:

```go
// variadic.go

package main

func simpleVariadicToSlice(numbers ...int) []int {
    return numbers
}

func mixedVariadicToSlice(name string, numbers ...int) (string, []int) {
```

```
      return name, numbers
}

// Does not work.
// func badVariadic(name ...string, numbers ...int) {}
```

We use the ... prefix before the data type to define a functions as a variadic function. Note that we can have only one variadic parameter per function and it has to be the last parameter. We can see this error if we uncomment the line for badVariadic and try to test the code.

variadic_test.go

We would like to test the two valid functions, simpleVariadicToSlice and mixedVariadicToSlice, for various rules defined in the previous section. However, for the sake of brevity, we will test these:

- simpleVariadicToSlice: This is for no arguments, three arguments, and also to look at how to pass a slice to a variadic function
- mixedVariadicToSlice: This is to accept a simple argument and a variadic argument

Let's now look at the code to test these two functions:

```
// variadic_test.go
package main

import "testing"

func TestSimpleVariadicToSlice(t *testing.T) {
    // Test for no arguments
    if val := simpleVariadicToSlice(); val != nil {
        t.Error("value should be nil", nil)
    } else {
        t.Log("simpleVariadicToSlice() -> nil")
    }

    // Test for random set of values
    vals := simpleVariadicToSlice(1, 2, 3)
    expected := []int{1, 2, 3}
    isErr := false
    for i := 0; i < 3; i++ {
        if vals[i] != expected[i] {
            isErr = true
```

```go
            break
        }
    }
    if isErr {
        t.Error("value should be []int{1, 2, 3}", vals)
    } else {
        t.Log("simpleVariadicToSlice(1, 2, 3) -> []int{1, 2, 3}")
    }

    // Test for a slice
    vals = simpleVariadicToSlice(expected...)
    isErr = false
    for i := 0; i < 3; i++ {
        if vals[i] != expected[i] {
            isErr = true
            break
        }
    }
    if isErr {
        t.Error("value should be []int{1, 2, 3}", vals)
    } else {
        t.Log("simpleVariadicToSlice([]int{1, 2, 3}...) -> []int{1, 2, 3}")
    }
}

func TestMixedVariadicToSlice(t *testing.T) {
    // Test for simple argument & no variadic arguments
    name, numbers := mixedVariadicToSlice("Bob")
    if name == "Bob" && numbers == nil {
        t.Log("Recieved as expected: Bob, <nil slice>")
    } else {
        t.Errorf("Received unexpected values: %s, %s", name, numbers)
    }
}
```

Running tests in variadic_test.go

Let's run these tests and see the output. We'll use the −v flag while running the tests to see the output of each individual test:

```
$ go test -v ./{variadic_test.go,variadic.go}
=== RUN   TestSimpleVariadicToSlice
--- PASS: TestSimpleVariadicToSlice (0.00s)
        variadic_test.go:10: simpleVariadicToSlice() -> nil
        variadic_test.go:26: simpleVariadicToSlice(1, 2, 3) -> []int{1, 2,
3}
```

```
        variadic_test.go:41: simpleVariadicToSlice([]int{1, 2, 3}...) ->
[]int{1, 2, 3}
=== RUN    TestMixedVariadicToSlice
--- PASS: TestMixedVariadicToSlice (0.00s)
        variadic_test.go:49: Received as expected: Bob, <nil slice>
PASS
ok      command-line-arguments  0.001s
```

addInt.go

The tests in `variadic_test.go` elaborated on the rules for the variadic function. However, you might have noticed that `TestSimpleVariadicToSlice` ran three tests in its function body, but `go test` treats it as a single test. Go provides a good way to run multiple tests within a single function, and we shall look them in `addInt_test.go`.

For this example, we will use a very simple function as shown in this code:

```
// addInt.go

package main

func addInt(numbers ...int) int {
    sum := 0
    for _, num := range numbers {
        sum += num
    }
    return sum
}
```

addInt_test.go

You might have also noticed in `TestSimpleVariadicToSlice` that we duplicated a lot of logic, while the only varying factor was the input and expected values. One style of testing, known as **Table-driven development**, defines a table of all the required data to run a test, iterates over the "rows" of the table and runs tests against them.

Let's look at the tests we will be testing against no arguments and variadic arguments:

```
// addInt_test.go

package main

import (
    "testing"
```

```go
)

func TestAddInt(t *testing.T) {
    testCases := []struct {
        Name     string
        Values   []int
        Expected int
    }{
        {"addInt() -> 0", []int{}, 0},
        {"addInt([]int{10, 20, 100}) -> 130", []int{10, 20, 100}, 130},
    }

    for _, tc := range testCases {
        t.Run(tc.Name, func(t *testing.T) {
            sum := addInt(tc.Values...)
            if sum != tc.Expected {
                t.Errorf("%d != %d", sum, tc.Expected)
            } else {
                t.Logf("%d == %d", sum, tc.Expected)
            }
        })
    }
}
```

Running tests in addInt_test.go

Let's now run the tests in this file, and we are expecting each of the row in the testCases table, which we ran, to be treated as a separate test:

```
$ go test -v ./{addInt.go,addInt_test.go}
=== RUN    TestAddInt
=== RUN    TestAddInt/addInt()_->_0
=== RUN    TestAddInt/addInt([]int{10,_20,_100})_->_130
--- PASS: TestAddInt (0.00s)
    --- PASS: TestAddInt/addInt()_->_0 (0.00s)
        addInt_test.go:23: 0 == 0
    --- PASS: TestAddInt/addInt([]int{10,_20,_100})_->_130 (0.00s)
        addInt_test.go:23: 130 == 130
PASS
ok      command-line-arguments  0.001s
```

nil_test.go

We can also create tests that are not specific to any particular source file; the only criteria is that the filename needs to have the `<text>_test.go` form. The tests in `nil_test.go` elucidate on some useful features of the language which the developer might find useful while writing tests. They are as follows:

- `httptest.NewServer`: Imagine the case where we have to test our code against a server that sends back some data. Starting and coordinating a full blown server to access some data is hard. The `http.NewServer` solves this issue for us.
- `t.Helper`: If we use the same logic to pass or fail a lot of `testCases`, it would make sense to segregate this logic into a separate function. However, this would skew the test run call stack. We can see this by commenting `t.Helper()` in the tests and rerunning `go test`.

We can also format our command-line output to print pretty results. We will show a simple example of adding a tick mark for passed cases and cross mark for failed cases.

In the test, we will run a test server, make GET requests on it, and then test the expected output versus actual output:

```go
// nil_test.go

package main

import (
    "fmt"
    "io/ioutil"
    "net/http"
    "net/http/httptest"
    "testing"
)

const passMark = "\u2713"
const failMark = "\u2717"

func assertResponseEqual(t *testing.T, expected string, actual string) {
    t.Helper() // comment this line to see tests fail due to 'if expected
!= actual'
    if expected != actual {
        t.Errorf("%s != %s %s", expected, actual, failMark)
    } else {
        t.Logf("%s == %s %s", expected, actual, passMark)
    }
}
```

```go
func TestServer(t *testing.T) {
    testServer := httptest.NewServer(
        http.HandlerFunc(
            func(w http.ResponseWriter, r *http.Request) {
                path := r.RequestURI
                if path == "/1" {
                    w.Write([]byte("Got 1."))
                } else {
                    w.Write([]byte("Got None."))
                }
            }))
    defer testServer.Close()

    for _, testCase := range []struct {
        Name     string
        Path     string
        Expected string
    }{
        {"Request correct URL", "/1", "Got 1."},
        {"Request incorrect URL", "/12345", "Got None."},
    } {
        t.Run(testCase.Name, func(t *testing.T) {
            res, err := http.Get(testServer.URL + testCase.Path)
            if err != nil {
                t.Fatal(err)
            }

            actual, err := ioutil.ReadAll(res.Body)
            res.Body.Close()
            if err != nil {
                t.Fatal(err)
            }
            assertResponseEqual(t, testCase.Expected, fmt.Sprintf("%s",
actual))
        })
    }
    t.Run("Fail for no reason", func(t *testing.T) {
        assertResponseEqual(t, "+", "-")
    })
}
```

Running tests in nil_test.go

We run three tests, where two test cases will pass and one will fail. This way we can see the tick mark and cross mark in action:

```
$ go test -v ./nil_test.go
=== RUN    TestServer
=== RUN    TestServer/Request_correct_URL
=== RUN    TestServer/Request_incorrect_URL
=== RUN    TestServer/Fail_for_no_reason
--- FAIL: TestServer (0.00s)
  --- PASS: TestServer/Request_correct_URL (0.00s)
        nil_test.go:55: Got 1. == Got 1. ✔
  --- PASS: TestServer/Request_incorrect_URL (0.00s)
        nil_test.go:55: Got None. == Got None. ✔
  --- FAIL: TestServer/Fail_for_no_reason (0.00s)
        nil_test.go:59: + != - ✘
FAIL
exit status 1
FAIL command-line-arguments 0.003s
```

Summary

In this chapter, we started by looking at the fundamental setup for running Go projects successfully. Then we looked at how to install dependencies for our Go projects and how to structure our project. We also looked at the important concepts behind Containers, what problems they solve, and how we will be using them in the book along with an example. Next, we looked at how to write tests in Go, and along the way, we learned a few interesting concepts when dealing with a variadic function and other useful test functions.

In the next chapter, we will start looking at one of the core fundamentals of Go programming—goroutines and the important details to keep in mind when using them.

2
Understanding Goroutines

Software development and programming has advanced quite a lot in the past decade. Many concepts that were previously considered academic and inefficient are beginning to find a place among modern software solutions. Two such concepts are coroutines (goroutines in Go) and channels. Conceptually, they have evolved over time and they have been implemented differently in each programming language. In many programming languages such as Ruby or Clojure, they are implemented as libraries, but in Go, they are implemented within the language as a native feature. As we shall see, this makes the language really modern, quite efficient, and an advanced programming language.

In this chapter we will try to gain an understanding of Go by looking at goroutines and the following topics:

- Concurrency and parallelism
- Go's runtime scheduler
- Gotchas when using goroutines

Concurrency and parallelism

Computer and software programs are useful because they do a lot of laborious work very fast and can also do multiple things at once. We want our programs to be able to do multiple things simultaneously, that is, multitask, and the success of a programming language can depend on how easy it is to write and understand multitasking programs.

Concurrency and parallelism are two terms that we are bound to come across often when looking into multitasking and they are often used interchangeably. However, they mean two distinctly different things.

The standard definitions given on the Go blog
(https://blog.golang.org/concurrency-is-not-parallelism) are as follows:

- **Concurrency**: *Concurrency is about dealing with lots of things at once*. This means that we manage to get multiple things done at once in a given period of time. However, we will only be doing a single thing at a time. This tends to happen in programs where one task is waiting and the program decides to run another task in the idle time. In the following diagram, this is denoted by running the yellow task in idle periods of the blue task.

- **Parallelism**: *Parallelism is about doing lots of things at once*. This means that even if we have two tasks, they are continuously working without any breaks in between them. In the diagram, this is shown by the fact that the green task is running independently and is not influenced by the red task in any manner:

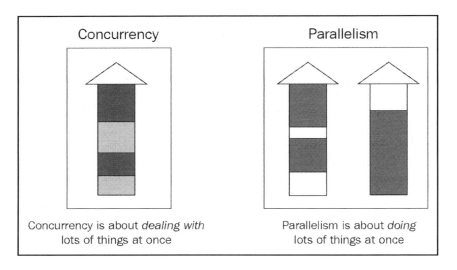

It is important to understand the difference between these two terms. Let's look at a few concrete examples to further elaborate upon the difference between the two.

Concurrency

Let's look at the concept of concurrency using a simple example of a few daily routine tasks and the way we can perform them.

Imagine you start your day and need to get six things done:

- Make hotel reservation
- Book flight tickets
- Order a dress
- Pay credit card bills
- Write an email
- Listen to an audiobook

The order in which they are completed doesn't matter, and for some of the tasks, such as writing an email or listening to an audiobook, you need not complete them in a single sitting. Here is one possible way to complete the tasks:

1. Order a dress.
2. Write one-third of the email.
3. Make hotel reservation.
4. Listen to 10 minutes of audiobook.
5. Pay credit card bills.
6. Write another one-third of the email.
7. Book flight tickets.
8. Listen to another 20 minutes of audiobook.
9. Complete writing the email.
10. Continue listening to audiobook until you fall asleep.

In programming terms, we have executed the above tasks **concurrently**. We had a complete day and we chose particular tasks from our list of tasks and started to work on them. For certain tasks, we even decided to break them up into pieces and work on the pieces between other tasks.

We will eventually write a program which does all of the preceding steps concurrently, but let's take it one step at a time. Let's start by building a program that executes the tasks sequentially, and then modify it progressively until it is purely concurrent code and uses goroutines. The progression of the program will be in three steps:

1. Serial task execution.
2. Serial task execution with goroutines.
3. Concurrent task execution.

Code overview

The code will consist of a set of functions that print out their assigned tasks as completed. In the cases of writing an email or listening to an audiobook, we further divide the tasks into more functions. This can be seen as follows:

- `writeMail, continueWritingMail1, continueWritingMail2`
- `listenToAudioBook, continueListeningToAudioBook`

Serial task execution

Let's first implement a program that will execute all the tasks in a linear manner. Based on the code overview we discussed previously, the following code should be straightforward:

```
package main

import (
    "fmt"
)

// Simple individual tasks
func makeHotelReservation() {
    fmt.Println("Done making hotel reservation.")
}
func bookFlightTickets() {
    fmt.Println("Done booking flight tickets.")
}
func orderADress() {
    fmt.Println("Done ordering a dress.")
}
func payCreditCardBills() {
    fmt.Println("Done paying Credit Card bills.")
}

// Tasks that will be executed in parts

// Writing Mail
func writeAMail() {
    fmt.Println("Wrote 1/3rd of the mail.")
    continueWritingMail1()
}
func continueWritingMail1() {
    fmt.Println("Wrote 2/3rds of the mail.")
    continueWritingMail2()
}
```

```
func continueWritingMail2() {
    fmt.Println("Done writing the mail.")
}

// Listening to Audio Book
func listenToAudioBook() {
    fmt.Println("Listened to 10 minutes of audio book.")
    continueListeningToAudioBook()
}
func continueListeningToAudioBook() {
    fmt.Println("Done listening to audio book.")
}

// All the tasks we want to complete in the day.
// Note that we do not include the sub tasks here.
var listOfTasks = []func(){
    makeHotelReservation, bookFlightTickets, orderADress,
    payCreditCardBills, writeAMail, listenToAudioBook,
}

func main() {
    for _, task := range listOfTasks {
        task()
    }
}
```

We take each of the main tasks and start executing them in simple sequential order. Executing the preceding code should produce unsurprising output, as shown here:

```
Done making hotel reservation.
Done booking flight tickets.
Done ordering a dress.
Done paying Credit Card bills.
Wrote 1/3rd of the mail.
Wrote 2/3rds of the mail.
Done writing the mail.
Listened to 10 minutes of audio book.
Done listening to audio book.
```

Serial task execution with goroutines

We took a list of tasks and wrote a program to execute them in a linear and sequential manner. However, we want to execute the tasks concurrently! Let's start by first introducing goroutines for the split tasks and see how it goes. We will only show the code snippet where the code actually changed here:

```
/*********************************************************************
   We start by making Writing Mail & Listening Audio Book concurrent.
 *********************************************************************/
// Tasks that will be executed in parts

// Writing Mail
func writeAMail() {
    fmt.Println("Wrote 1/3rd of the mail.")
    go continueWritingMail1()  // Notice the addition of 'go' keyword.
}
func continueWritingMail1() {
    fmt.Println("Wrote 2/3rds of the mail.")
    go continueWritingMail2()  // Notice the addition of 'go' keyword.
}
func continueWritingMail2() {
    fmt.Println("Done writing the mail.")
}

// Listening to Audio Book
func listenToAudioBook() {
    fmt.Println("Listened to 10 minutes of audio book.")
    go continueListeningToAudioBook()  // Notice the addition of 'go'
keyword.
}
func continueListeningToAudioBook() {
    fmt.Println("Done listening to audio book.")
}
```

The following is a possible output:

```
Done making hotel reservation.
Done booking flight tickets.
Done ordering a dress.
Done paying Credit Card bills.
Wrote 1/3rd of the mail.
Listened to 10 minutes of audio book.
```

Whoops! That's not what we were expecting. The output from the `continueWritingMail1`, `continueWritingMail2`, and `continueListeningToAudioBook` functions is missing; the reason being that we are using goroutines. Since goroutines are not waited upon, the code in the `main` function continues executing and once the control flow reaches the end of the `main` function, the program ends. What we would really like to do is to wait in the `main` function until all the goroutines have finished executing. There are two ways we can do this—using channels or using `WaitGroup`. Since we have Chapter 3, *Channels and Messages*, dedicated to channels, let's use `WaitGroup` in this section.

In order to use `WaitGroup`, we have to keep the following in mind:

- Use `WaitGroup.Add(int)` to keep count of how many goroutines we will be running as part of our logic.
- Use `WaitGroup.Done()` to signal that a goroutine is done with its task.
- Use `WaitGroup.Wait()` to wait until all goroutines are done.
- Pass `WaitGroup` instance to the goroutines so they can call the `Done()` method.

Based on these points, we should be able to modify the source code to use `WaitGroup`. The following is the updated code:

```
package main

import (
    "fmt"
    "sync"
)

// Simple individual tasks
func makeHotelReservation(wg *sync.WaitGroup) {
    fmt.Println("Done making hotel reservation.")
    wg.Done()
}
func bookFlightTickets(wg *sync.WaitGroup) {
    fmt.Println("Done booking flight tickets.")
    wg.Done()
}
func orderADress(wg *sync.WaitGroup) {
    fmt.Println("Done ordering a dress.")
    wg.Done()
}
func payCreditCardBills(wg *sync.WaitGroup) {
    fmt.Println("Done paying Credit Card bills.")
    wg.Done()
```

```go
}

// Tasks that will be executed in parts

// Writing Mail
func writeAMail(wg *sync.WaitGroup) {
    fmt.Println("Wrote 1/3rd of the mail.")
    go continueWritingMail1(wg)
}
func continueWritingMail1(wg *sync.WaitGroup) {
    fmt.Println("Wrote 2/3rds of the mail.")
    go continueWritingMail2(wg)
}
func continueWritingMail2(wg *sync.WaitGroup) {
    fmt.Println("Done writing the mail.")
    wg.Done()
}

// Listening to Audio Book
func listenToAudioBook(wg *sync.WaitGroup) {
    fmt.Println("Listened to 10 minutes of audio book.")
    go continueListeningToAudioBook(wg)
}
func continueListeningToAudioBook(wg *sync.WaitGroup) {
    fmt.Println("Done listening to audio book.")
    wg.Done()
}

// All the tasks we want to complete in the day.
// Note that we do not include the sub tasks here.
var listOfTasks = []func(*sync.WaitGroup){
    makeHotelReservation, bookFlightTickets, orderADress,
    payCreditCardBills, writeAMail, listenToAudioBook,
}

func main() {
    var waitGroup sync.WaitGroup
    // Set number of effective goroutines we want to wait upon
    waitGroup.Add(len(listOfTasks))

    for _, task := range listOfTasks{
        // Pass reference to WaitGroup instance
        // Each of the tasks should call on WaitGroup.Done()
        task(&waitGroup)
    }
    // Wait until all goroutines have completed execution.
    waitGroup.Wait()
}
```

Here is one possible output order; notice how `continueWritingMail1` and `continueWritingMail2` were executed at the end after `listenToAudioBook` and `continueListeningToAudioBook`:

```
Done making hotel reservation.
Done booking flight tickets.
Done ordering a dress.
Done paying Credit Card bills.
Wrote 1/3rd of the mail.
Listened to 10 minutes of audio book.
Done listening to audio book.
Wrote 2/3rds of the mail.
Done writing the mail.
```

Concurrent task execution

In the final output of the previous section, we can see that all the tasks in `listOfTasks` are being executed in serial order, and the last step for maximum concurrency would be to let the order be determined by Go runtime instead of the order in `listOfTasks`. This might sound like a laborious task, but in reality this is quite simple to achieve. All we need to do is add the `go` keyword in front of `task(&waitGroup)`:

```
func main() {
    var waitGroup sync.WaitGroup
    // Set number of effective goroutines we want to wait upon
    waitGroup.Add(len(listOfTasks))

    for _, task := range listOfTasks {
        // Pass reference to WaitGroup instance
        // Each of the tasks should call on WaitGroup.Done()
        go task(&waitGroup) // Achieving maximum concurrency
    }

    // Wait until all goroutines have completed execution.
    waitGroup.Wait()
```

Following is a possible output:

```
Listened to 10 minutes of audio book.
Done listening to audio book.
Done booking flight tickets.
Done ordering a dress.
Done paying Credit Card bills.
Wrote 1/3rd of the mail.
Wrote 2/3rds of the mail.
```

```
Done writing the mail.
Done making hotel reservation.
```

If we look at this possible output, the tasks were executed in the following order:

1. Listen to audiobook.
2. Book flight tickets.
3. Order a dress.
4. Pay credit card bills.
5. Write an email.
6. Make hotel reservations.

Now that we have a good idea on what concurrency is and how to write concurrent code using `goroutines` and `WaitGroup`, let's dive into parallelism.

Parallelism

Imagine that you have to write a few emails. They are going to be long and laborious, and the best way to keep yourself entertained is to listen to music while writing them, that is, listening to music "in parallel" to writing the emails. If we wanted to write a program that simulates this scenario, the following is one possible implementation:

```
package main

import (
    "fmt"
    "sync"
    "time"
)

func printTime(msg string) {
    fmt.Println(msg, time.Now().Format("15:04:05"))
}

// Task that will be done over time
func writeMail1(wg *sync.WaitGroup) {
    printTime("Done writing mail #1.")
    wg.Done()
}
func writeMail2(wg *sync.WaitGroup) {
    printTime("Done writing mail #2.")
    wg.Done()
}
```

```
func writeMail3(wg *sync.WaitGroup) {
    printTime("Done writing mail #3.")
    wg.Done()
}

// Task done in parallel
func listenForever() {
    for {
        printTime("Listening...")
    }
}

func main() {
    var waitGroup sync.WaitGroup
    waitGroup.Add(3)

    go listenForever()

    // Give some time for listenForever to start
    time.Sleep(time.Nanosecond * 10)

    // Let's start writing the mails
    go writeMail1(&waitGroup)
    go writeMail2(&waitGroup)
    go writeMail3(&waitGroup)

    waitGroup.Wait()
}
```

The output of the program might be as follows:

```
Done writing mail #3. 19:32:57
Listening... 19:32:57
Listening... 19:32:57
Done writing mail #1. 19:32:57
Listening... 19:32:57
Listening... 19:32:57
Done writing mail #2. 19:32:57
```

The numbers represent the time in terms of Hour:Minutes:Seconds and, as can be seen, they are being executed in parallel. You might have noticed that the code for parallelism looks almost identical to the code for the final concurrency example. However, in the function listenForever, we are printing Listening... in an infinite loop. If the preceding example was written without goroutines, the output would keep printing Listening... and never reach the writeMail function calls.

Now that we understand how goroutine can be used to run concurrent programs, let's look at how Go is allowing us to do this. We shall next look at the scheduler used by Go runtime.

Go's runtime scheduler

The Go program, along with the runtime, is managed and executed on multiple OS threads. The runtime uses a scheduler strategy known as **M:N** scheduler, which will schedule M number of goroutines on N number of OS threads. As a result, whenever we need to run or switch to a different goroutine, the context switching will be fast, and this also enables us to use multiple cores of the CPU for parallel computing.

A solid understanding of Go's runtime and scheduler would be quite interesting and useful, and now would be a good time to look at them in detail.

From the Go scheduler's perspective, there are primarily three entities:

- Goroutine (G)
- OS thread or machine (M)
- Context or processor (P)

Let's look at what they do. We will also be looking the partial struct definitions of these entities to provide a better idea of how scheduling is implemented and how it works.

Goroutine

It is the logical unit of execution that contains the actual instructions for our program/functions to run. It also contains other important information regarding the goroutine, such as the stack memory, which machine (M) it is running on, and which Go function called it. The following are some of the elements in the goroutine struct that might come in handy for this section:

```
// Denoted as G in runtime
type g struct {
    stack          stack // offset known to runtime/cgo
    m              *m    // current m; offset known to arm liblink
    goid           int64
    waitsince      int64  // approx time when the g become blocked
    waitreason string  // if status==Gwaiting
    gopc           uintptr // pc of go statement that created this goroutine
    startpc        uintptr // pc of goroutine function
    timer          *timer  // cached timer for time.Sleep
```

```
    // ...
}
```

An interesting thing to know is that when our Go program starts, a goroutine called main goroutine is first launched, and it takes care of setting up the runtime space before starting our program. A typical runtime setup might include things such as maximum stack size, enabling garbage collector, and so on.

OS thread or machine

Initially, the OS threads or machines are created by and managed by the OS. Later on, the scheduler can request for more OS threads or machines to be created or destroyed. It is the actual resource upon which a goroutine will be executed. It also maintains information about the main goroutine, the G currently being run on it, **thread local storage (tls)**, and so on:

```
// Denoted as M in runtime
type m struct {
    g0              *g          // goroutine with scheduling stack
    tls             [6]uintptr // thread-local storage (for x86 extern
register)
    curg            *g          // current running goroutine
    p               puintptr   // attached p for executing go code (nil
if not executing go code)
    id              int32
    createstack [32]uintptr // stack that created this thread.
    spinning        bool        // m is out of work and is actively looking
for work

    // ...
}
```

Context or processor

We have a global scheduler which takes care of bringing up new M, registering G, and handling system calls. However, it does not handle the actual execution of goroutines. This is done by an entity called **Processor**, which has its own internal scheduler and a queue called runqueue (`runq` in code) consisting of goroutines that will be executed in the current context. It also handles switching between various goroutines and so on:

```
// Denoted as P in runtime code
type p struct {
    id      int32
    m       muintptr // back-link to associated m (nil if idle)
    runq [256]guintptr

    //...
}
```

From Go 1.5 onwards, a Go runtime can have a maximum number of GOMAXPROCS Ps running at any given point in the program's lifetime. Of course, we can change this number by either setting the GOMAXPROCS environment variable or by calling the GOMAXPROCS() function.

Scheduling with G, M, and P

By the time the program is ready to start executing, the runtime has machines and processors set up. The runtime would request the OS to start an ample number of Machines (M), GOMAXPROCS number of Processors to execute goroutines (G). It is important to understand that M is the actual unit of execution and G is the logical unit of execution. However, they require P to actually execute G against the M. Let's look at a possible scenario to better explain the scheduling process. First let's look at the components we shall be using for the scenario:

- We have a set of M ready to run: M1...Mn
- We also have two Ps: P1 and P2 with runqueues—runq1 and runq2 respectively
- Last but not least, we also have 20 goroutines, G1...G20, which we want to execute as part of the program

Go's runtime and all of the components, M1...Mn, P1 and P2, and G1...G20, are represented as shown in the following figure:

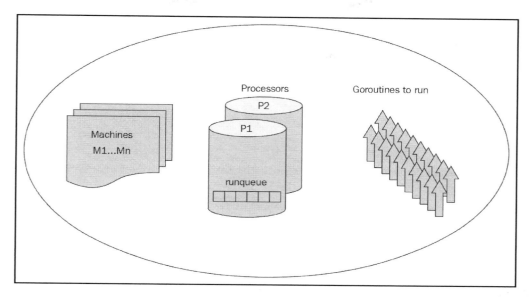

Given that we have two Processors, the global scheduler would ideally distribute the goroutines between the two Processors equally. Assume that P1 is assigned to work on G1...G10 and and puts them into its runqueue, and similarly P2 puts G11...G20 in its runqueue. Next, P1's scheduler pops a goroutine from its runqueue to run, G1, picks a machine to run it on, M1, and similarly P2 runs G11 on M2. This can be illustrated by the following diagram:

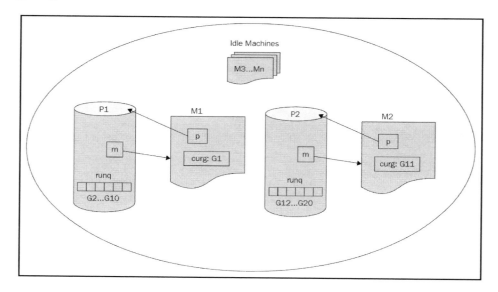

A process's internal scheduler is also responsible for switching out the current goroutine with the next one that it wants to execute. If everything is going well, the scheduler will switch the current goroutine for one of three possible reasons:

- Time slice for current execution is over: A process will use **schedtick** (it is incremented every time the scheduler is called) to keep track of how long the current goroutine has been executing and, once a certain time limit is reached, the current goroutine will be put back in the runqueue and the next goroutine is picked up for execution.
- Done with execution: Simply put, the goroutine is done executing all of its instructions. In this case, it will not be put back in the runqueue.
- Waiting on system call: In some cases, the goroutine might need to make a system system call, and as a result, the goroutine will be blocked. Given that we have a handful of processors, it doesn't make sense to block such an expensive resource. The good news is that in Go, the processor is not required to wait on the system call; instead it can leave the waiting M and G combo, which will be picked up by the global scheduler after the system call. In the meantime, the processor can pick another M from the available machines, pick another goroutine from its runqueue, and start executing it. This is explained with the help of the following diagram:

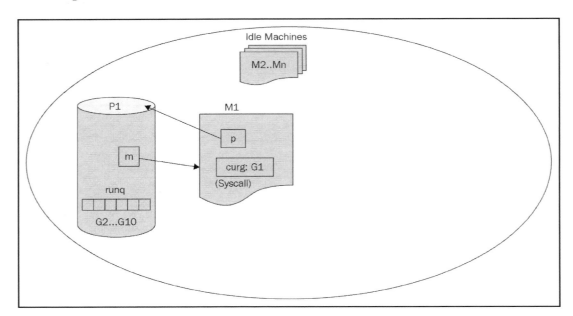

The previous diagram explains that the processor P1 is running goroutine G1 on machine M1. G1 will now begin making a system call. This can be illustrated in the following diagram:

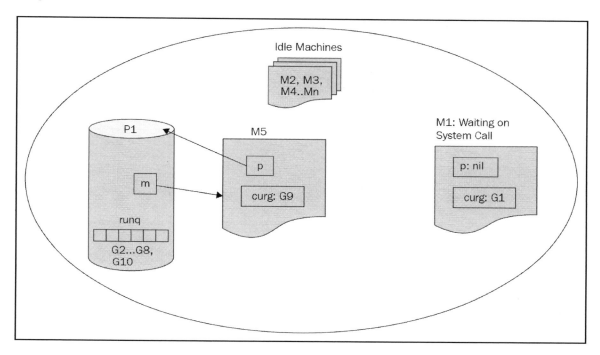

The previous diagram explains that the processor P1 detaches itself from machine M1 and goroutine G1 due to a system call. P1 picks a new machine, M5, and a new goroutine, G9, to execute:

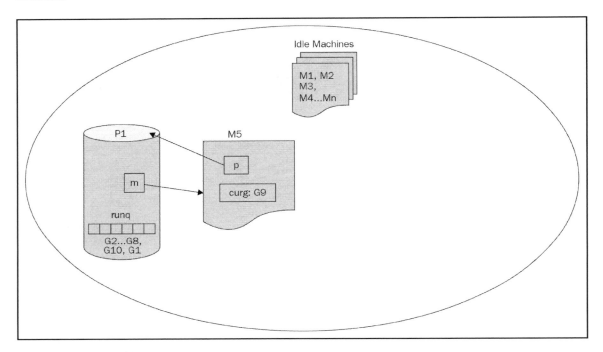

In the previous diagram, the G1-M1 system call is completed. Now G1 is put back in the P1 runqueue and M1 is added to the set of idle machines.

In the last part of this section, we are going to discuss another strategy implemented in the scheduler, called **work-stealing**.

Let's say that processor P1 has 10 goroutines and P2 has 10 goroutines. However, it turns out that the goroutines in P1 were quickly completed and now there are zero goroutines in P1's runqueue. It would be a tragedy if P1 were idle and waiting for the global scheduler to provide it with more work. With the help of the work-stealing strategy, P1 starts checking with other processors and, if another processor has goroutines in its runqueue, it will "steal" half of them and start executing them. This ensures that we are maximizing the CPU usage for our program. Let's ask two interesting questions:

- What if a processor realizes that it can't steal any more tasks? The procesor will wait for a little while expecting new goroutines and, if none are created, the processor is killed.
- Can a processor steal more than half of a runqueue? Even if we have many processors at work, work-stealing will always take half of the target processor's runqueue.

This can be illustrated with the following diagram:

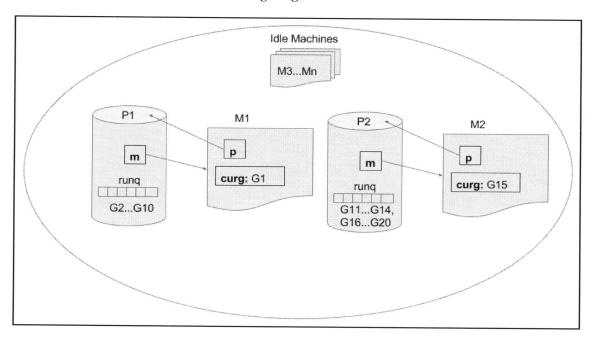

The preceding diagram shows two processors, P1 and P2, executing a goroutine each from their runqueue on two machines. Let's consider that the tasks for processor P2 complete while P1 is running. This is shown in the figure here:

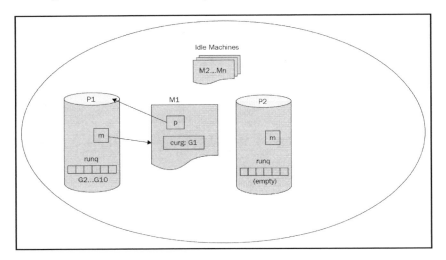

Processor P2 has exhausted its runqueue, and does not have any more goroutines to execute. Thanks to the work-stealing strategy, P2 has "stolen" half of the goroutines from P1's runqueue and can start executing them, as shown in the figure here:

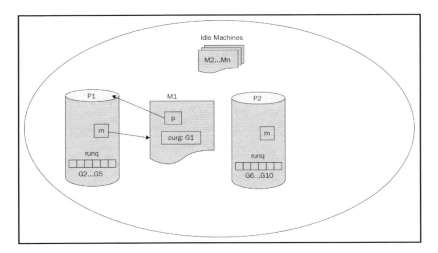

Gotchas when using goroutines

By this point, we should have developed a good understanding of how goroutines and the scheduler works. Let's now look at a few things that may catch us by surprise while working with goroutines.

Single goroutine halting the complete program

We know that goroutines run across multiple threads and multiple cores. So what happens when we have a panic in one of the threads? Here is an example that would let us simulate such a situation. We will create a lot of similar goroutines, whose sole purpose is to take a number and divide it by itself after subtracting 10 from the denominator. This will work fine for the majority of cases, except when the number is 10. The following code implements the described functionality:

```go
package main

import (
    "fmt"
    "sync"
)

func simpleFunc(index int, wg *sync.WaitGroup) {
    // This line should fail with Divide By Zero when index = 10
    fmt.Println("Attempting x/(x-10) where x = ", index, " answer is : ",
index/(index-10))
    wg.Done()
}

func main() {
    var wg sync.WaitGroup
    wg.Add(40)
    for i := 0; i < 40; i += 1 {
        go func(j int) {
            simpleFunc(j, &wg)
        }(i)
    }

    wg.Wait()
}
```

The output of the previous code can be as follows:

```
Attempting x/(x-10) where x =  39  answer is :  1
Attempting x/(x-10) where x =  20  answer is :  2...
Attempting x/(x-10) where x =  37  answer is :  1
Attempting x/(x-10) where x =  11  answer is :  11
panic: runtime error: integer divide by zerogoroutine 15
[running]:main.simpleFunc(0xa, 0xc42000e280)
...exit status 2
```

Essentially, a lot of goroutines were put in the runqueue, and upon being executed in random order, their outputs were printed to the console. However, as soon as the goroutine with index = 10 was executed, it raised a panic which was not handled by the function, and this resulted in the complete program halting and exiting with status code 2. This shows that even a single error or panic that hasn't been handled will halt the complete program!

However, it wouldn't make sense to crash the program because we faced a panic that we might have been able to handle graciously. Go allows us to recover from a panic with an appropriately named function called recover. Let's look at how to use recover in the previous code example:

```
package main

import (
    "fmt"
    "sync"
)

func simpleFunc(index int, wg *sync.WaitGroup) {
    // functions with defer keyword are executed at the end of the function
    // regardless of whether the function was executed successfully or not.
    defer func() {
        if r := recover(); r != nil {
            fmt.Println("Recovered from", r)
        }
    }()

    // We have changed the order of when wg.Done is called because
    // we should call upon wg.Done even if the following line fails.
    // Whether a defer function exists or not is dependent on whether it is
registered
    // before or after the failing line of code.
    defer wg.Done()
    // This line should fail with Divide By Zero when index = 10
    fmt.Println("Attempting x/(x-10) where x = ", index, " answer is : ",
index/(index-10))
```

```
    }

func main() {
    var wg sync.WaitGroup
    wg.Add(40)
    for i := 0; i < 40; i += 1 {
        go func(j int) {
            simpleFunc(j, &wg)
        }(i)
    }

    wg.Wait()
}
```

The output for the preceding code can be as follows:

```
Attempting x/(x-10) where x =  39  answer is :  1
Attempting x/(x-10) where x =  14  answer is :  3
Recovered from runtime error: integer divide by zero
Attempting x/(x-10) where x =  3  answer is :  0
...Attempting x/(x-10) where x =  29  answer is :  1
Attempting x/(x-10) where x =  9  answer is :  -9
```

Goroutines aren't predictable

In this chapter, we started by looking at how Go enables us to write code that is concurrent and, to an extent, parallel. Then we followed up with a discussion on how Go schedules goroutines over machines and processors. It is possible that we might be able to reason how the goroutines are going to be distributed over machines and processors, which in turn might let us write non-standard or hacky Go code.

Consider the code from the *Parallelism* section, where we tried to simulate listening to music while writing a few emails. Here is the output of the code for quick reference:

```
Done writing mail #3. 19:32:57
Listening... 19:32:57
Listening... 19:32:57
Done writing mail #1. 19:32:57
Listening... 19:32:57
Listening... 19:32:57
Done writing mail #2. 19:32:57
```

We can now easily infer that there were at least two Ps, and one of them was being used by the goroutine printing `Listening...`, while the other P was handling the goroutines related to writing emails.

This is all well and good, however consider the case where GOMAXPROCS is set to 1 or the system has low hardware capabilities which might result in fewer machines. It is possible that this might lead to the goroutine printing Listening... run forever and never giving control to the other goroutines. In reality, the Go compiler should detect this case and accordingly plan the scheduling of goroutines. However, it would be better to plan our code so that we do not have to rely on Go's scheduler and its current implementation.

Summary

Goroutines are concurrent and, to an extent, parallel; however, we should think of them as being concurrent. The order of execution of goroutines is not predictable and we should not rely on them to be executed in any particular order.

We should also take care to handle errors and panics in our goroutines because even though they are being executed in parallel, a panic in one goroutine will crash the complete program. Finally, goroutines can block on system calls, however this will not block the execution of the program nor slow down the performance of the overall program.

We looked at a few of the design concepts behind Go's runtime scheduler to understand why all of this happens.

You might be wondering why we haven't discussed channels in this chapter. The reason is that by not relying on channels we were able to look at goroutines in their most elemental form. This allowed us to dive deeper into the concept and implementation of goroutines.

In the next chapter, we shall be looking at channels and how they further empower goroutines.

3
Channels and Messages

In Chapter 2, *Understanding Goroutines*, we looked at how goroutines work, how to use them in a concurrent fashion, and some of the common mistakes that might occur. They were simple to use and reason about, but they were limited because they are able to spawn other goroutines and wait on system calls. In reality, goroutines are more capable than what was shown in the previous chapter, and to uncover their full potential we need to understand how to use channels, which is the aim of the current chapter. Here, we will look at the following topics:

- Controlling parallelism
- Channels and data communication
- Types of channels
- Closing and multiplexing channels

Controlling parallelism

We know that spawned goroutines will start executing as soon as possible and in a simultaneous fashion. However, there is an inherent risk involved when the said goroutines need to work on a common source that has a lower limit on the number of simultaneous tasks it can handle. This might cause the common source to significantly slow down or in some cases even fail. As you might guess, this is not a new problem in the field of computer science, and there are many ways to handle it. As we shall see throughout the chapter, Go provides mechanisms to control parallelism in a simple and intuitive fashion. Let's start by looking at an example to simulate the problem of burdened common source, and then proceed to solve it.

Imagine a cashier who has to process orders, but has a limit to process only 10 orders in a day. Let's look at how to present this as a program:

```go
// cashier.go
package main

import (
    "fmt"
    "sync"
)

func main() {
    var wg sync.WaitGroup
    // ordersProcessed & cashier are declared in main function
    // so that cashier has access to shared state variable
'ordersProcessed'.
    // If we were to declare the variable inside the 'cashier' function,
    // then it's value would be set to zero with every function call.
    ordersProcessed := 0
    cashier := func(orderNum int) {
        if ordersProcessed < 10 {
            // Cashier is ready to serve!
            fmt.Println("Processing order", orderNum)
            ordersProcessed++
        } else {
            // Cashier has reached the max capacity of processing orders.
            fmt.Println("I am tired! I want to take rest!", orderNum)
        }
        wg.Done()
    }

    for i := 0; i < 30; i++ {
        // Note that instead of wg.Add(60), we are instead adding 1
        // per each loop iteration. Both are valid ways to add to WaitGroup
as long as we can ensure the right number of calls.
        wg.Add(1)
        go func(orderNum int) {
            // Making an order
            cashier(orderNum)
        }(i)

    }
    wg.Wait()
}
```

A possible output of the program might be as follows:

```
Processing order 29
Processing order 22
Processing order 23
Processing order 13
Processing order 24
Processing order 25
Processing order 21
Processing order 26
Processing order 0
Processing order 27
Processing order 14
I am tired! I want to take rest! 28
I am tired! I want to take rest! 1
I am tired! I want to take rest! 7
I am tired! I want to take rest! 8
I am tired! I want to take rest! 2
I am tired! I want to take rest! 15
...
```

The preceding output shows a cashier who was overwhelmed after taking 10 orders. However, an interesting point to note is that if you run the preceding code multiple times, you might get different outputs. For example, all of the 30 orders might be processed in one of the runs!

This is happening because of what is known as the **race condition**. A data race (or race condition) occurs when multiple actors (goroutines, in our case) are trying to access and modify a common shared state, and this results in incorrect reads and writes by the goroutines.

We can try to solve this issue in two ways:

- Increasing the limit for processing orders
- Increasing the number of cashiers

Increasing the limit is feasible only to a certain extent, beyond which it would start degrading the system or in the case of the cashier, work will neither be efficient nor 100% accurate. On the contrary, by increasing the number of cashiers, we can start processing more orders consecutively while not changing the limit. There are two approaches to this:

- Distributed work without channels
- Distributed work with channels

Distributed work without channels

In order to distribute the work equally among the cashiers, we need to know the amount of orders we will get beforehand and ensure that the work each cashier receives is within his/her limit. This is not the most practical solution, because it would fail in a real-world scenario where we would need to keep track of how many orders each cashier has processed and divert the remaining orders to the other cashiers. However, before we look at the correct way to solve it, let's take time to better understand the problem of uncontrolled parallelism and try to solve it. The following code attempts to solve it in a naïve manner, which should provide us with a good start:

```go
// wochan.go

package main

import (
    "fmt"
    "sync"
)

func createCashier(cashierID int, wg *sync.WaitGroup) func(int) {
    ordersProcessed := 0
    return func(orderNum int) {
        if ordersProcessed < 10 {
            // Cashier is ready to serve!
            //fmt.Println("Cashier ", cashierID, "Processing order",
orderNum, "Orders Processed", ordersProcessed)
            fmt.Println(cashierID, "->", ordersProcessed)
            ordersProcessed++
        } else {
            // Cashier has reached the max capacity of processing
orders.
            fmt.Println("Cashier ", cashierID, "I am tired! I want to
take rest!", orderNum)
        }
        wg.Done()
    }
}

func main() {
    cashierIndex := 0
    var wg sync.WaitGroup

    // cashier{1,2,3}
    cashiers := []func(int){}
    for i := 1; i <= 3; i++ {
```

```
        cashiers = append(cashiers, createCashier(i, &wg))
    }

    for i := 0; i < 30; i++ {
        wg.Add(1)

        cashierIndex = cashierIndex % 3

        func(cashier func(int), i int) {
            // Making an order
            go cashier(i)
        }(cashiers[cashierIndex], i)

        cashierIndex++
    }
    wg.Wait()
}
```

The following is one possible output:

```
Cashier  2 Processing order 7
Cashier  1 Processing order 6
Cashier  3 Processing order 8
Cashier  3 Processing order 29
Cashier  1 Processing order 9
Cashier  3 Processing order 2
Cashier  2 Processing order 10
Cashier  1 Processing order 3
. . .
```

We split the available 30 orders between cashiers 1, 2, and 3, and all of the orders were successfully processed without anyone complaining about being tired. However, note that the code to make this work required a lot of work on our end. We had to create a function generator to create cashiers, keep track of which cashier to use via cashierIndex, and so on. And the worst part is that the preceding code isn't correct! Logically, it might seem to be doing what we want; however, note that we are spawning multiple goroutines that are working on variables with a shared state, ordersProcessed! This is the race condition we discussed earlier. The good news is that we can detect it in wochan.go in two ways:

- In createCashier function, replace fmt.Println("Cashier ", cashierID, "Processing order", orderNum) with fmt.Println(cashierID, "->", ordersProcessed). Here is one possible output:

```
3 -> 0
3 -> 1
1 -> 0
```

```
. . .
2 -> 3
3 -> 1  # Cashier 3 sees ordersProcessed as 1 but three lines above,
Cashier 3
was at ordersProcessed == 4!
3 -> 5
1 -> 4
1 -> 4 # Cashier 1 sees ordersProcessed == 4 twice.
2 -> 4
2 -> 4 # Cashier 2 sees ordersProcessed == 4 twice.
. . .
```

- The previous point proves that the code is not correct; however, we had to guess the possible issue in the code and then verify it. Go provides us with tools to detect data race so that we do not have to worry about such issues. All we have to do to detect data race is to test, run, build, or install the package (file in the case of run) with the −race flag . Let's run this on our program and look at the output:

```
$ go run −race wochan.go
Cashier  1 Processing order 0
Cashier  2 Processing order 1
==================
WARNING: DATA RACE
Cashier  3 Processing order 2
Read at 0x00c4200721a0 by goroutine 10:
main.createCashier.func1()
    wochan.go:11 +0x73
Previous write at 0x00c4200721a0 by goroutine 7:
main.createCashier.func1()
    wochan.go:14 +0x2a7
Goroutine 10 (running) created at:
main.main.func1()
    wochan.go:40 +0x4a
main.main()
    wochan.go:41 +0x26e
Goroutine 7 (finished) created at:
main.main.func1()
    wochan.go:40 +0x4a
main.main()
    wochan.go:41 +0x26e
==================
Cashier  2 Processing order 4
Cashier  3 Processing order 5
==================
WARNING: DATA RACE
Read at 0x00c420072168 by goroutine 9:
main.createCashier.func1()
```

```
        wochan.go:11 +0x73
Previous write at 0x00c420072168 by goroutine 6:
main.createCashier.func1()
        wochan.go:14 +0x2a7
Goroutine 9 (running) created at:
main.main.func1()
        wochan.go:40 +0x4a
main.main()
        wochan.go:41 +0x26e
Goroutine 6 (finished) created at:
main.main.func1()
        wochan.go:40 +0x4a
main.main()
        wochan.go:41 +0x26e
==================
Cashier  1 Processing order 3
Cashier  1 Processing order 6
Cashier  2 Processing order 7
Cashier  3 Processing order 8
...
Found 2 data race(s)
exit status 66
```

As can be seen, the -race flag helped us to detect the data race.

Does this mean that we cannot distribute our tasks when we have shared state? Of course we can! But we need to use mechanisms provided by Go for this purpose:

- Mutexes, semaphores, and locks
- Channels

Mutex is a mutual exclusion lock that provides us with a synchronization mechanism to allow only one goroutine to access a particular piece of code or shared state at any given point in time. As already stated, for synchronization problems, we can use either mutex or channels, and Go recommends using the right construct for the right job. However, in practice, using channels provides us with a higher level of abstraction and greater versatility in terms of usage, though mutex has its uses. It is for this reason for that, throughout this chapter and the book, we will be making use of channels.

Distributed work with channels

We are certain about three things now: we want to distribute our orders among the cashiers correctly, we want to ensure that the correct number of orders are processed by each cashier, and we want to use channels to solve this problem. Before we address how to solve the cashier problem using channels, let's first look at the basic syntax and usage of a channel.

What is a channel?

A channel is a communication mechanism that allows us to pass data between goroutines. It is an in-built data type in Go. Data can be passed using one of the primitive data types or we can create our own complex data type using structs.

Here is a simple example to demonstrate how to use a channel:

```
// simchan.go
package main

import "fmt"

// helloChan waits on a channel until it gets some data and then prints the
value.
func helloChan(ch <- chan string) {
    val := <- ch
    fmt.Println("Hello, ", val)
}

func main() {
    // Creating a channel
    ch := make(chan string)

    // A Goroutine that receives data from a channel
    go helloChan(ch)

    // Sending data to a channel.
    ch <- "Bob"
}
```

If we run the preceding code, it would print the following output:

```
Hello, Bob
```

The basic pattern for using channels can be explained by the following steps:

1. Create the channel to accept the data to be processed.
2. Launch the goroutines that are waiting on the channel for data.
3. Then, we can either use `main` function or other goroutines to pass data into the channel.
4. The goroutines listening on the channel can accept the data and process them .

The advantage of using channels is that multiple goroutines can wait on the same channel and execute tasks concurrently.

Solving the cashier problem with goroutines

Before we try to solve the problem, let's first formulate what we want to achieve:

1. Create a channel `orderChannel` that accepts all orders.
2. Launch the required number of cashier goroutines that accept limited numbers of orders from `orderChannel`.
3. Start putting all orders into `orderChannel`.

Let's look at one possible solution that tries to solve the cashier problem using the preceding steps:

```go
// wichan.go
package main

import (
    "fmt"
    "sync"
)

func cashier(cashierID int, orderChannel <-chan int, wg *sync.WaitGroup) {
    // Process orders upto limit.
    for ordersProcessed := 0; ordersProcessed < 10; ordersProcessed++ {
        // Retrieve order from orderChannel
        orderNum := <-orderChannel
        // Cashier is ready to serve!
        fmt.Println("Cashier ", cashierID, "Processing order", orderNum,
"Orders Processed", ordersProcessed)
        wg.Done()
    }
}
```

```
func main() {
    var wg sync.WaitGroup
    wg.Add(30)
    ordersChannel := make(chan int)

    for i := 0; i < 3; i++ {
        // Start the three cashiers
        func(i int) {
            go cashier(i, ordersChannel, &wg)
        }(i)
    }
    // Start adding orders to be processed.
    for i := 0; i < 30; i++ {
        ordersChannel <- i
    }
    wg.Wait()
}
```

On running the preceding code with –race flag, we can see that the code ran without any data races:

```
$ go run -race wichan.go
Cashier  2 Processing order 2 Orders Processed 0
Cashier  2 Processing order 3 Orders Processed 1
Cashier  0 Processing order 0 Orders Processed 0
Cashier  1 Processing order 1 Orders Processed 0
...
Cashier  0 Processing order 27 Orders Processed 9
```

The code is quite straightforward, is easy to parallelize, and works well without causing any data races.

Channels and data communication

Go is a statically typed language, and this means that a given channel can only send or receive data of a single data type. In Go's terminology, this is known as a channel's **element type**. A Go channel will accept any valid Go data type including functions. Here is an example of a simple program that accepts and calls on functions:

```
// elems.go
package main

import "fmt"

func main() {
```

```go
// Let's create three simple functions that take an int argument
fcn1 := func(i int) {
    fmt.Println("fcn1", i)
}
fcn2 := func(i int) {
    fmt.Println("fcn2", i*2)
}
fcn3 := func(i int) {
    fmt.Println("fcn3", i*3)
}

ch := make(chan func(int)) // Channel that sends & receives functions
that take an int argument
done := make(chan bool)    // A Channel whose element type is a boolean
value.

// Launch a goroutine to work with the channels ch & done.
go func() {
    // We accept all incoming functions on Channel ch and call the
functions with value 10.
    for fcn := range ch {
        fcn(10)
    }
    // Once the loop terminates, we print Exiting and send true to done
Channel.
    fmt.Println("Exiting")
    done <- true
}()

// Sending functions to channel ch
ch <- fcn1
ch <- fcn2
ch <- fcn3

// Close the channel once we are done sending it data.
close(ch)

// Wait on the launched goroutine to end.
<-done
}
```

The output of the preceding code is as follows:

```
fcn1 10
fcn2 20
fcn3 30
Exiting
```

In the preceding code sample, we say that the channel `ch` has the element type of `func(int)` and the channel `done` has the element type of `bool`. There are a lot more interesting details in the code, but we shall discuss them in the following sections.

Messages and events

So far we have been using the term *data* to refer to the values that are being sent and received from a channel. While this might be easy to understand so far, Go uses two specific terms to describe the type of data that is being communicated over the channels. They are called **messages** and **events**. In terms of code they are identical, but the terms are used to help us understand the *type* of data that is being sent. In a nutshell:

- Messages are generally values we want the goroutine to process and act on them if required.
- Events are used to signify that a certain *event* has occurred. The actual value received might not be as important as the act of receiving a value. Note that though we use the term *event*, they are still a type of *message*.

In the previous code example, values sent to `ch` are messages, while the value sent to `done` is an event. An important point to note is that element types of event channels tend to be `struct{}{}`, `bool`, or `int`.

Now that we understand what channel element types, messages, and events are, let's look at the different types of channels.

Types of channels

Go provides us with three major variations on channel types. They can be broadly classified into:

- Unbuffered
- Buffered
- Unidirectional (send-only and receive-only type channels)

The unbuffered channel

This is the basic channel type available in Go. It is quite straightforward to use—we send data into the channel and we receive data at the other end. The interesting part is that any goroutine operating on an unbuffered channel will be blocked until both the sender and receiver goroutines are available. For example, consider the following code snippet:

```
ch := make(chan int)
go func() {ch <- 100}      // Send 100 into channel.
                           Channel: send100
go func() {val := <- ch}   // Goroutine waiting on channel.
                           Channel: recv1
go func() {val := <- ch}   // Another goroutine waiting on channel.
                           Channel: recv2
```

We have a channel `ch` of element type `int`. We start three goroutines; one sends a message of `100` onto the channel (`send100`) and the other two goroutines (`recv1` and `recv2`) wait on the channel. `send100` is blocked until either of `recv1` or `recv2` starts listening on the channel to receive the message. If we assume that `recv2` receives the message sent on the channel by `send100`, then `recv1` will be waiting until another message is sent on the channel. If the preceding four lines are the only communications on the channel, then `recv1` will wait until the program ends and then will be abruptly killed off by the Go runtime.

The buffered channel

Consider the case where we are able to send more messages into a channel than the goroutines receiving the messages can handle them. If we use unbuffered channels, it would significantly slow down the program because we will have to wait for each message to be processed before we can put in another message. It would be ideal if the channel could store these extra messages or "buffer" the messages. This is exactly what a buffered channel does. It maintains a queue of messages which a goroutine will consume at its own pace. However, even a buffered channel has a limited capacity; we need to define the capacity of the queue at the time of channel creation.

So, how do we use a buffered channel? Syntax-wise, it is identical to using an unbuffered channel. The behavior of a buffer channel can be explained as follows:

- **If a buffered channel is empty**: Receiving messages on the channel is blocked until a message is sent across the channel
- **If a buffered channel is full**: Sending messages on the channel is blocked until at least one message is received from the channel, thus making space for the new message to be put on the channel's buffer or queue
- **If a buffered channel is partially filled, that is, neither full nor empty**: Either sending or receiving messages on a channel is unblocked and the communication is instantaneous

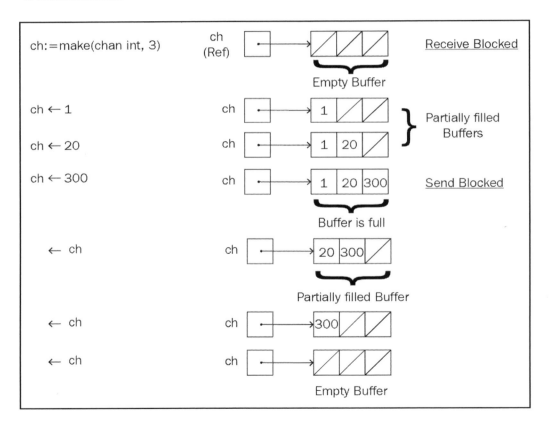

Communication over a buffered channel

The unidirectional buffer

Messages can be sent and received from a channel. However, when goroutines use channels for communication, they are generally going to be for a single purpose: either to send or receive from a channel. Go allows us to specify whether a channel being used by a goroutine is for sending or receiving messages. It accomplishes this with the help of unidirectional channels. Once a channel has been identified as being unidirectional, we cannot perform the other operation on them. This means that a unidirectional send channel cannot be used to receive messages, and a unidirectional receive channel cannot be used to send messages. Any attempts to do so would be caught by the Go compiler as compile-time errors.

Here is an example of using unidirectional channels correctly:

```go
// unichans.go
package main

import (
    "fmt"
    "sync"
)

func recv(ch <-chan int, wg *sync.WaitGroup) {
    fmt.Println("Receiving", <-ch)
    wg.Done()
}

func send(ch chan<- int, wg *sync.WaitGroup) {
    fmt.Println("Sending...")
    ch <- 100
    fmt.Println("Sent")
    wg.Done()
}

func main() {
    var wg sync.WaitGroup
    wg.Add(2)

    ch := make(chan int)
    go recv(ch, &wg)
    go send(ch, &wg)

    wg.Wait()
}
```

The expected output would be as follows:

```
Sending...
Receiving 100      # (or) Sent
Sent               # (or) Receiving 100
```

Now, let's try to send over a receiving channel and see what happens. We will only see the changed function in the previous example here:

```
// unichans2.go
// ...
// Changed function
func recv(ch <-chan int, wg *sync.WaitGroup) {
    fmt.Println("Receiving", <-ch)
    fmt.Println("Trying to send") // signalling that we are going to send
over channel.
    ch <- 13                      // Sending over channel
    wg.Done()
}
```

Now, if we try to run or build the updated program, we will get the following error:

```
$ go run unichans.go
# command-line-arguments
unichans.go:11: invalid operation: ch <- 13 (send to receive-only type <-
chan int)
```

So, how would the program behave if we used a buffered channel? Since there will be no blocking on an unfilled channel, the send goroutine sends a message onto the channel and then continues executing. The recv goroutine reads from the channel when it starts executing and then prints it:

```
// buffchan.go
package main

import (
    "fmt"
    "sync"
)

func recv(ch <-chan int, wg *sync.WaitGroup) {
    fmt.Println("Receiving", <-ch)
    wg.Done()
}

func send(ch chan<- int, wg *sync.WaitGroup) {
    fmt.Println("Sending...")
```

```
        ch <- 100
        fmt.Println("Sent")
        wg.Done()
}

func main() {
        var wg sync.WaitGroup
        wg.Add(2)

        // Using a buffered channel.
        ch := make(chan int, 10)
        go recv(ch, &wg)
        go send(ch, &wg)

        wg.Wait()
}
```

The output would be as follows:

```
Sending...
Sent
Receiving 100
```

Closing channels

In the previous sections, we have looked at three types of channels and how to create them. In this section, let's look at how to close the channels and how this might affect sending and receiving on these channels. We close a channel when we no longer want to send any messages on the said channel. How a channel behaves after being closed is different for each type of channel. Let's dive into them:

- **Unbuffered closed channel**: Sending messages will cause panic and receiving on it will yield an immediate zero value of the channel's element type.
- **Buffered closed channel**: Sending messages will cause panic but receiving on it will first yield all the values in the channel's queue. Once the queue has been exhausted, then the channel will start yielding zero values of the channel's element type.

The following is a program to elucidate on the two preceding points:

```
// closed.go
package main

import "fmt"
```

```
type msg struct {
    ID    int
    value string
}

func handleIntChan(intChan <-chan int, done chan<- int) {
    // Even though there are only 4 elements being sent via channel, we
retrieve 6 values.
    for i := 0; i < 6; i++ {
        fmt.Println(<-intChan)
    }
    done <- 0
}

func handleMsgChan(msgChan <-chan msg, done chan<- int) {
    // We retrieve 6 values of element type struct 'msg'.
    // Given that there are only 4 values in the buffered channel,
    // the rest should be zero value of struct 'msg'.
    for i := 0; i < 6; i++ {
        fmt.Println(fmt.Sprintf("%#v", <-msgChan))
    }
    done <- 0
}

func main() {
    intChan := make(chan int)
    done := make(chan int)

    go func() {
        intChan <- 9
        intChan <- 2
        intChan <- 3
        intChan <- 7
        close(intChan)
    }()
    go handleIntChan(intChan, done)

    msgChan := make(chan msg, 5)
    go func() {
        for i := 1; i < 5; i++ {
            msgChan <- msg{
                ID:    i,
                value: fmt.Sprintf("VALUE-%v", i),
            }
        }
        close(msgChan)
    }()
    go handleMsgChan(msgChan, done)
```

```
    // We wait on the two channel handler goroutines to complete.
    <-done
    <-done

    // Since intChan is closed, this will cause a panic to occur.
    intChan <- 100
}
```

The following is one possible output of the program:

```
9
2
3
7
0
0
main.msg{ID:1, value:"VALUE-1"}
main.msg{ID:2, value:"VALUE-2"}
main.msg{ID:3, value:"VALUE-3"}
main.msg{ID:4, value:"VALUE-4"}
main.msg{ID:0, value:""}
main.msg{ID:0, value:""}
panic: send on closed channel
goroutine 1 [running]:
main.main()
        closed.go:58 +0x194
    Process finished with exit code 2
```

Finally, here are some further useful points about closing channels and closed channels:

- It is not possible to determine if a channel has been closed. The best we can do is check if we were able to successfully retrieve a message from a channel. We know that the default syntax for retrieving on channel is `msg := <- ch`. However, there is a variant on this retrieval: `msg, ok := <-ch`. The second parameter tells us if the retrieval was successful. If a channel is closed, `ok` will be `false`. This can be used to tell when a channel has been closed.

- `msg, ok := <-ch` is a common pattern when iterating over channels. As a result, Go allows us to `range` over a channel. When a channel closes, the `range` loop ends.

- Closing a closed channel, nil channel, or a receive-only channel will cause panic. Only a bidirectional channel or send-only channel can be closed.

- It is not mandatory to close a channel and irrelevant for the **garbage collector (GC)**. If the GC determines that a channel is unreachable, irrespective of whether it is open or closed, the channel will be garbage collected.

Multiplexing channels

Multiplexing describes the methodology where we use a single resource to act upon multiple signals or actions. This method is used extensively in telecommunications and computer networks. We might find ourselves in a situation where we have multiple types of tasks that we want to execute. However, they can only be executed in mutual exclusion, or they need to work on a shared resource. For this, we make use of a pattern in Go known as channels multiplexing. Before we dive into how to actually multiplex channels, let's try to implement it on our own.

Imagine that we have a set of channels and we want to act on them as soon as data is sent over a channel. Here's a naïve approach on how we want to do this:

```go
// naiveMultiplexing.go
package main

import "fmt"

func main() {
    channels := [5](chan int){
        make(chan int),
        make(chan int),
        make(chan int),
        make(chan int),
        make(chan int),
    }

    go func() {
        // Starting to wait on channels
        for _, chX := range channels {
            fmt.Println("Receiving from", <- chX)
        }
    }()

    for i := 1; i < 6; i++ {
        fmt.Println("Sending on channel:", i)
        channels[i] <- 1
    }
}
```

The output of the preceding program is as follows:

```
Sending on channel: 1
fatal error: all goroutines are asleep - deadlock!
goroutine 1 [chan send]:
main.main()
        /home/entux/Documents/Code/GO-WORKSPACE/src/distributed-
go/ch3/naiveSwitch.go:23 +0x2b1
goroutine 5 [chan receive]:
main.main.func1(0xc4200160c0, 0xc420016120, 0xc420016180, 0xc4200161e0,
0xc420016240)
        GO-WORKSPACE/src/distributed-go/ch3/naiveSwitch.go:17 +0xba
created by main.main
        GO-WORKSPACE/src/distributed-go/ch3/naiveSwitch.go:19 +0x18b
```

In the loop within the goroutine, the first channel is never waited upon and this causes the deadlock in the goroutine. Multiplexing helps us wait upon multiple channels without blocking on any of the channels while acting on a message once it is available on a channel.

The following are some important points to remember when multiplexing on channels:

- **Syntax:**

```
select {
case <- ch1:
  // Statements to execute if ch1 receives a message
case val := <- ch2:
  // Save message received from ch2 into a variable and
  execute statements for ch2
}
```

- It is possible that, by the time `select` is executed, more than one case is ready with a message. In this case, `select` will not execute all of the cases, but will pick one at random, execute it, and then exit the `select` statement.
- However, the preceding point might be limited if we want to react on messages being sent to all channels in `select` cases. Then we can put the `select` statement inside a `for` loop and it will ensure that all messages will be handled.
- Even though the `for` loop will handle messages sent on all channels, the loop will still be blocked until a message is available on it. There might be scenarios where we do not wish to block the loop iteration and instead do some "default" action. This can be achieved using `default` case in `select` statement.

- Updated syntax based on the preceding two points is:

```
for {
  select {
      case <- ch1:
      // Statements to execute if ch1 receives a message
      case val := <- ch2:
      // Save message received from ch2 into a variable and
      execute statements for ch2
      default:
      // Statements to execute if none of the channels has yet
      received a message.
  }
}
```

- In the case of buffered channels, the order in which the messages are received is not guaranteed.

The following is the correct way to multiplex on all the required channels without being blocked on any and continuing to work on all the messages being sent:

```
// multiplexing.go

package main

import (
    "fmt"
)

func main() {
    ch1 := make(chan int)
    ch2 := make(chan string)
    ch3 := make(chan int, 3)
    done := make(chan bool)
    completed := make(chan bool)

    ch3 <- 1
    ch3 <- 2
    ch3 <- 3
    go func() {
        for {

            select {
                case <-ch1:
                    fmt.Println("Received data from ch1")
                case val := <-ch2:
                    fmt.Println(val)
```

```
                case c := <-ch3:
                        fmt.Println(c)
                case <-done:
                        fmt.Println("exiting...")
                        completed <- true
                        return
            }
        }
    }()

    ch1 <- 100
    ch2 <- "ch2 msg"
    // Uncomment us to avoid leaking the 'select' goroutine!
    //close(done)
    //<-completed
}
```

The following is the output of the preceding program:

```
1
Received data from ch1
2
3
```

Unfortunately, there is one flaw with the program: it leaks the goroutine handling, `select`. This is also pointed out in the comment near the end of the `main` function. This generally happens when we have a goroutine that is running but we cannot directly reach it. Even if a goroutine's reference is not stored, the GC will not garbage collect it. Thus, we need a mechanism to stop and return from such goroutines. In general, this can be achieved by creating a channel specifically for returning from the goroutine.

In the preceding code, we send the signal via the `done` channel. The following would be the output if we uncomment the lines and then run the program:

```
1
2
3
Received data from ch1
ch2 msg
exiting...
```

Summary

In this chapter, we looked at the reason to control parallelism and developed an appreciation for the complexity of the task when a shared state is involved. We used the example of an overworked cashier as a programming problem to solve and to experiment with channels, and further explored different types of channels and the nuances involved with using them. For example, we saw that both closed buffered and unbuffered channels will cause panic if we try to send messages on them, and receiving messages from them leads to different results based on whether the channel is buffered and if the channel is empty or full. We also saw how to wait on multiple channels without blocking on any with the help of `select`.

In later chapters, from `Chapter 5`, *Introducing Goophr*, through to `Chapter 8`, *Deploying Goophr*, we will be developing a distributed web application. This requires us to have basic knowledge of how to interact with a web server, using the HTTP protocol using tools other than a web browser. This knowledge will come in handy not only when interacting with our application but also with the standard web as a developer. This will be the subject of the next chapter, `Chapter 4`, *The RESTful Web*, where we will look at the tools and protocols we will be using to interact with our web application.

4
The RESTful Web

In the previous chapters, we looked at two of the most important components of Go—goroutines and channels. In the following chapters, we will build a distributed application using Go, and it is very important to understand how to write applications for the internet or, in our case, the web. In this chapter, we shall look at a particular way of building web applications using the REST web protocol. We shall also look at how to interact with a REST-based web application. We shall be covering them in the following manner:

- A brief look at HTTP and sessions
- Fundamentals to build a REST server
- Design a simple REST server
- Tools to interact with a REST server

HTTP and sessions

In this section we will take a brief look at the HTTP protocol and how it has evolved over time. Also discuss how servers keep track of user state using HTTP sessions. This knowledge will come in handy when we try to understand how REST protocol works.

A brief history of HTTP

In order to better understand the advantages of the REST protocol, let us take a small detour into how the internet was used before the REST web protocol came onto the scene. The internet in 1990s was mostly used to store and share documents as marked up documents using **HTTP (Hypertext Transfer Protocol)**. For this chapter, HTTP can be summarized as follows:

- HTTP is a network communication protocol that starts with an HTTP request and ends with an HTTP response.
- HTTP responses during the early periods consisted of plain text documents, but soon the HTML format gained traction as it allowed for more stylized documents.
- Web browsers brought in a new age of internet: merely displaying text documents with different font weights wasn't enough. CSS and JavaScript came to the fore to make these documents customizable and more interactive. All these advancements led to what we now call the *web*.
- One could interact with a web server using a URL and an HTTP method. There are nine HTTP methods, but, for the purpose of this book, we are only interested in five of them:
  - GET: This is used when sending simple HTTP requests
  - POST : This is used when we want to include valuable information while sending HTTP requests
  - PUT, PATCH, and DELETE: Technically, they are identical to, POST method, although they differ in functionally

We shall revisit these HTTP methods in the next section and explore them in greater detail.

HTTP sessions

The HTTP protocol in itself is stateless; that is, it has no idea of what is accessing a web page, who can POST to a page, and so on. For the majority of HTTP servers during this period (1990s), they could be thought of as file server; that is, they serve static files over the internet. However, the modern web experience is more expansive. Consider visiting Gmail or Facebook, and the website knows who we are and we are shown customized content that is dynamically generated for us. They maintain the "state" of which article we are reading or the mail we are writing. If we were to close the browser and return to the website after a while, it can drop us right back to where we left off. Given that the HTTP protocol and HTTP servers are stateless, how do these websites keep track of all these things and link them back to the correct user? The answer is an HTTP session.

When we log onto a website from a browser, we provide it with credentials to identify ourselves. The server responds back with a response that also consists of a token, which will be used to identify us in the near future. The token can be in the form of a session ID, cookie, authentication header, and so on. A web server maintains a table of such tokens and the corresponding user IDs. After we have logged onto a website, the browser always sends the corresponding token in the headers to the server with every request. As a result, the web server is able to keep track of each user and show correct content to any given user. How does the server do this? It maintains all the state information on the server side!

The REST protocol

Even in the 1990s, the computers and internet technology kept advancing rapidly and the web browsers kept evolving simultaneously. This meant that the web servers themselves could start offloading some of the work to the web client; that is, the web browser. Slowly this began to lead developers to experiment with different software architectures for developing web applications. By 2010, the REST protocol became the most prevalent way to design a modern web application.

REST (Representation State Transfer Protocol) was first described by *Roy Fielding* in his seminal paper titled, *Architectural Styles and the Design of Network-based Software Architectures* (`https://www.ics.uci.edu/~fielding/pubs/dissertation/fielding_dissertation.pdf`). This way of designing a web application has many advantages. It is practical, efficient in CPU usage and network load, scales better for increasing internet traffic, and so on. The following are some of the properties and benefits of using REST software architecture.

The server and client architecture

In the *HTTP sessions* section, we described a server that was doing most of the work and browser was responsible for relaying user inputs to the server, parsing the HTML document returned back from the server, and rendering it in the browser for the user. REST allows us to split the application into a server and client. A server (backend) is responsible for executing business logic, and a client (frontend) is responsible for communicating user interaction to the server. It might sound like not much has changed; however, the remaining properties of REST architecture will be more apparent.

The standard data format

REST revolves around the communication state and data between the backend and frontend using a standard data format. This results in the decoupling of backend and frontend. This means that we are no longer bound to using only a web browser to communicate with the server, and this in turn means that our servers are now capable of being used to interact with web applications, command-line applications, and so on. REST allows us to use any type of data format for communication, although JSON format has become the lingua franca for communication over REST protocol.

Resources

Since our frontend and backend are separate, we need to communicate the state and data between the two. In the frontend, we will need to show all available entities for the service we are providing. These entities are called **resources**.

Consider a server that provides us with a REST interface (REST API) that has a list of books in our personal library. In this case, *list of books* are resources and we can request information about each of them from the backend at particular endpoints. For our example, the endpoint can be `<URL>/api/books`. `/api` prefix is a convention generally used in REST applications to express that we are interacting with the backend URLs. The resources can generally be thought of as a collection of data, like rows of a database table.

Reusing the HTTP protocol

We defined endpoints in the previous subsection, *Resources*, but how do we interact with them? REST is built on top of the HTTP protocol and it uses HTTP methods, or verbs in the case of REST, to interact with the server. Let's take our endpoint from the previous example, `/api/books`, to understand how it is used.

GET

REST uses the `GET` verb to retrieve items of the specific resource type. Given that we have a lot of items, it is possible to retrieve a specific resource item and to retrieve all the available resource items. Retrieval of a specific resource item is generally done by providing the id of the item. The following shows the two forms of `GET` used for retrieval:

- `/api/books`: This returns a list of all books in the library
- `/api/books/<id>` : This returns information about a particular book in the library

POST

REST uses the `POST` verb to create a new item of the specific resource type. Resource creation might require extra information, which is provided in the body of the `POST` request. The information being provided as part of the body has to be in the data format the REST server can handle. POSTing to `/api/books` signifies that we want to add a new book to the list of books in our library.

PUT and PATCH

These take the form `/api/books/<id>`. These methods are only applicable for an already existing resource. They will update a given resource with the data or new state of the resource provided in the request's body. `PUT` expects a resource's new state to be provided in completion, including fields that haven't changed. `PATCH` can be thought of as a more relaxed version of `PUT` because we do not need to provide the complete new state but only the fields that need to be updated.

DELETE

REST uses the `DELETE` verb to remove a specific resource item. It takes the form of `/api/resource/<id>`. It deletes a particular resource based on `<id>`. REST supports deletion of all items of a given resource type, although this doesn't make sense as it is now possible for a user to accidentally delete all items of the resource type. For this and many other reasons, no server actually implements this feature.

Upgradable components

Consider the case where we need to make changes to the UI and this is not going to affect the server logic. If a website was not split according to client and server architecture, we would have to upgrade the complete website and this would be quite a time-consuming task. Thanks to the split of frontend and backend, we can make changes and upgrade only the required system. Thus, we can ensure minimal disruption of service.

Fundamentals of a REST server

Now that we have an understanding of how a REST application should behave, let's build one! We shall start out by first building a simple web server, then design the books REST server by describing design decisions and API definitions, and finally build a REST server based on the design.

A simple web server

Go provides us with an inbuilt library for building web servers, `net/http`. For every endpoint we want to create on our server, we have to do two things:

1. Create a handler function for the endpoint, which accepts two parameters, one for writing to response and one to handle the incoming Request.
2. Register the endpoint using `net/http.HandleFunc`.

The following is a simple web server that accepts all incoming requests, logs them on to the console, and then returns a `Hello, World!` message.

```
// helloServer.go

package main
```

```go
import (
    "fmt"
    "log"
    "net/http"
)

func helloWorldHandler(w http.ResponseWriter, r *http.Request) {
    msg := fmt.Sprintf("Received request [%s] for path: [%s]", r.Method,
r.URL.Path)
    log.Println(msg)

    response := fmt.Sprintf("Hello, World! at Path: %s", r.URL.Path)
    fmt.Fprintf(w, response)
}

func main() {
    http.HandleFunc("/", helloWorldHandler) // Catch all Path

    log.Println("Starting server at port :8080...")
    http.ListenAndServe(":8080", nil)
}
```

Here are some sample requests and responses when requesting the URL in the browser:

```
http://localhost:8080/   --> Hello, World! at Path: /
http://localhost:8080/asdf  htt--> Hello, World! at Path: /asdf
http://localhost:8080/some-path/123   --> Hello, World! at Path: /some-
path/123
```

And the following is the server output:

```
2017/10/03 13:35:46 Starting server at port :8080...
2017/10/03 13:36:01 Received request [GET] for path: [/]
2017/10/03 13:37:22 Received request [GET] for path: [/asdf]
2017/10/03 13:37:40 Received request [GET] for path: [/some-path/123]
```

Notice that even though we have provided multiple paths, they are all defaulting to the / path.

Designing a REST API

We have looked at the history behind HTTP and the core concepts behind the REST protocol. We built a simple web server to show some of the server-side code needed to build a REST server. It is time for us to design and build a REST server using everything we have learned so far.

We will start by defining the data format for our REST API, and then we will create a web server that works as per the REST API specifications we defined.

The data format

In this section, we will describe the format of the book resource, and then we will start defining each of the REST API interactions as well as the expected result from these interactions.

The book resource

The following is the basic definition of a book resource. It is a JSON array with the format `"<key>": "<value-type>"`, though the actual entities used in the application will consist of real values:

```
{
    "id": "string",
    "title": "string",
    "link": "string"
}
```

GET /api/books

This REST API call will retrieve a list of all items of the book resource type. The response's JSON format in our example consists of an array of the book resource type. However, this return format is not the only way to return items. An alternate but more popular format consists of a JSON object with key "data" that consists of the actual results and any further keys that the server might want to send back in the response.

Let's now look at the simple format we will be using in our example:

```
// Request
GET "<URL>/api/books/"

// Response
[
  {
    "id": "1",
    "title": "book1",
    "link": "http://link-to-book-1.com"
  },
  {
    "id": "2",
    "title": "book2",
```

```
        "link": "http://link-to-book-2.com"
    }
  ]
```

GET /api/books/<id>

This form of the GET call will retrieve a single book resource item based on the <id> provided. In general the response's JSON object will be of the defined resource type, though a server might decide to add or remove certain fields based on the service's logic. For our API, we will return all the fields defined in our resource type.

Let's look at an example when we try to retrieve a book resource with id "1":

```
// Request
GET "<URL>/api/books/1"

// Response
{
    "id": "1",
    "title": "book1",
    "link": "http://link-to-book-1.com"
}
```

POST /api/books

This REST API call will create a new item of book resource type. However, in order to create a new item, we would need to provide all the necessary data. It is possible to have POST requests that do not require any extra information. But in our case, we need to send information such as the title and link to the book as request's payload.

In this example, we want to create a book item with the title "book5" and link "http://link-to-book5.com". Note that since our server already has two items of the book resource type, the new item is created with id of "3"; this is the implementation as per our server. Other REST servers might behave differently.

```
// Request
POST "<URL>/api/books"

// payload
{
    "title": "book5",
    "link": "http://link-to-book-5.com"
}

// response
```

```
{
  "id": "3",
  "title": "book5",
  "link": "http://link-to-book-5.com"
}
```

PUT /api/books/<id>

We will use PUT in our REST API to update a specific resource type. PUT defined in our API is stringent with accepting the payload without complete data, that is, it will reject with incomplete payloads.

In this example, we will modify the newly created book "3" and change its link to point at "http://link-to-book-15.com":

```
// Request
PUT "<URL>/api/books/3"

// payload
{
  "title": "book5",
  "link": "http://link-to-book-15.com"
}

// response
{
  "id": "3",
  "title": "book5",
  "link": "http://link-to-book-15.com"
}
```

DELETE /api/books/<id>

This is the REST API call used to delete a specific book resource. This kind of request doesn't need a body and only requires the book id as part of the URL as shown in the next example.

In this example, we will delete book 2. Note that we do not return anything in response; other REST servers might return the deleted item:

```
// Request
DELETE "<URL>/api/books/2"

// Response
[]
```

Unsuccessful requests

It is possible that we could send ill-constructed requests, requests on unavailable entities, or bad incomplete payloads. For all such instances, we will send relevant HTTP error codes. Depending upon a server's implementation, it is possible to return a single error code. Some servers return a standard error code "404" for added security to not let malicious users try to find items of resource type they do not own.

Design decisions

We have defined our REST API and next we would like to implement the server. It is important to formulate what we want our server to accomplish before writing any code. The following are some of the specifications for the server:

- We need to extract <id> for PUT, DELETE, and single resource GET Requests.
- We want to log every incoming request similar to the helloWorldHandler.
- It would be tedious and bad coding practice to duplicate so much effort. We can make use of closures and function literals to create new functions for us that will combine the tasks from previous two points.
- In order to keep the example simple, we shall be using a map[string]bookResource to store the state of all book resources. All operations will be done on this map. In real-world servers, we would generally be using a database to store these resources.
- Go server can handle concurrent requests, and this means that we should ensure that the map of book resources is safe from race conditions.

Let's look at what the code might look like based on the design we came up with.

The REST server for books API

We have divided our program as follows:

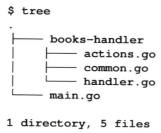

```
$ tree
.
├────── books-handler
│       ├────── actions.go
│       ├────── common.go
│       └────── handler.go
└────── main.go

1 directory, 5 files
```

Now let's look at the source code of each file.

main.go

The `main.go` source file consists of code mostly responsible for assembling and running the web server. The logic to actually respond to HTTP requests are distributed across other files:

```go
// restServer/main.go

package main

import (
    "fmt"
    "log"
    "net/http"

    booksHandler "github.com/last-ent/distributed-go/chapter4/books-handler"
)

func main() {
    // Get state (map) for books available on REST server.
    books := booksHandler.GetBooks()
    log.Println(fmt.Sprintf("%+v", books))
    actionCh := make(chan booksHandler.Action)

    // Start goroutine responsible for handling interaction with the books map
    go booksHandler.StartBooksManager(books, actionCh)

    http.HandleFunc("/api/books/",
booksHandler.MakeHandler(booksHandler.BookHandler, "/api/books/",
actionCh))

    log.Println("Starting server at port 8080...")
    http.ListenAndServe(":8080", nil)
}
```

books-handler/common.go

The code in this source file is generic logic, which might be shared across multiple requests:

 It is generally a good practice to identify the logic that is not tied to one particular handler and then move it into common.go or similar source files, as this would make them easier to find and reduce duplicated code.

```go
// restServer/books-handler/common.go

package booksHandler

import (
    "encoding/json"
    "fmt"
    "log"
    "net/http"
)

// bookResource is used to hold all data needed to represent a Book
resource in the books map.
type bookResource struct {
    Id     string 'json:"id"'
    Title string 'json:"title"'
    Link   string 'json:"link"'
}

// requestPayload is used to parse request's Payload. We ignore Id field
for simplicity.
type requestPayload struct {
    Title string 'json:"title"'
    Link   string 'json:"link"'
}

// response struct consists of all the information required to create the
correct HTTP response.
type response struct {
    StatusCode int
    Books       []bookResource
}

// Action struct is used to send data to the goroutine managing the state
(map) of books.
// RetChan allows us to send data back to the Handler function so that we
can complete the HTTP request.
type Action struct {
```

```go
    Id      string
    Type    string
    Payload requestPayload
    RetChan chan<- response
}

// GetBooks is used to get the initial state of books represented by a map.
func GetBooks() map[string]bookResource {
    books := map[string]bookResource{}
    for i := 1; i < 6; i++ {
        id := fmt.Sprintf("%d", i)
        books[id] = bookResource{
            Id:    id,
            Title: fmt.Sprintf("Book-%s", id),
            Link:  fmt.Sprintf("http://link-to-book%s.com", id),
        }
    }
    return books
}

// MakeHandler shows a common pattern used reduce duplicated code.
func MakeHandler(fn func(http.ResponseWriter, *http.Request, string,
string, chan<- Action),
    endpoint string, actionCh chan<- Action) http.HandlerFunc {

    return func(w http.ResponseWriter, r *http.Request) {
        path := r.URL.Path
        method := r.Method

        msg := fmt.Sprintf("Received request [%s] for path: [%s]", method,
path)
        log.Println(msg)

        id := path[len(endpoint):]
        log.Println("ID is ", id)
        fn(w, r, id, method, actionCh)
    }
}

// writeResponse uses the pattern similar to MakeHandler.
func writeResponse(w http.ResponseWriter, resp response) {
    var err error
    var serializedPayload []byte

    if len(resp.Books) == 1 {
        serializedPayload, err = json.Marshal(resp.Books[0])
    } else {
        serializedPayload, err = json.Marshal(resp.Books)
```

```
    }

    if err != nil {
        writeError(w, http.StatusInternalServerError)
        fmt.Println("Error while serializing payload: ", err)
    } else {
        w.Header().Set("Content-Type", "application/json")
        w.WriteHeader(resp.StatusCode)
        w.Write(serializedPayload)
    }
}

// writeError allows us to return error message in JSON format.
func writeError(w http.ResponseWriter, statusCode int) {
    jsonMsg := struct {
        Msg   string 'json:"msg"'
        Code int    'json:"code"'
    }{
        Code: statusCode,
        Msg:  http.StatusText(statusCode),
    }

    if serializedPayload, err := json.Marshal(jsonMsg); err != nil {
        http.Error(w, http.StatusText(http.StatusInternalServerError),
http.StatusInternalServerError)
        fmt.Println("Error while serializing payload: ", err)
    } else {
        w.Header().Set("Content-Type", "application/json")
        w.WriteHeader(statusCode)
        w.Write(serializedPayload)
    }
}
```

books-handler/actions.go

This source file consists of functions to handle each of the HTTP request's method calls:

```
// restServer/books-handler/actions.go

package booksHandler

import (
    "net/http"
)

// actOn{GET, POST, DELETE, PUT} functions return Response based on
specific Request type.
```

```go
func actOnGET(books map[string]bookResource, act Action) {
    // These initialized values cover the case:
    // Request asked for an id that doesn't exist.
    status := http.StatusNotFound
    bookResult := []bookResource{}

    if act.Id == "" {

        // Request asked for all books.
        status = http.StatusOK
        for _, book := range books {
            bookResult = append(bookResult, book)
        }
    } else if book, exists := books[act.Id]; exists {

        // Request asked for a specific book and the id exists.
        status = http.StatusOK
        bookResult = []bookResource{book}
    }

    act.RetChan <- response{
        StatusCode: status,
        Books:      bookResult,
    }
}

func actOnDELETE(books map[string]bookResource, act Action) {
    book, exists := books[act.Id]
    delete(books, act.Id)

    if !exists {
        book = bookResource{}
    }

    // Return the deleted book if it exists else return an empty book.
    act.RetChan <- response{
        StatusCode: http.StatusOK,
        Books:      []bookResource{book},
    }
}

func actOnPUT(books map[string]bookResource, act Action) {
    // These initialized values cover the case:
    // Request asked for an id that doesn't exist.
    status := http.StatusNotFound
    bookResult := []bookResource{}

    // If the id exists, update its values with the values from the
```

```
payload.
    if book, exists := books[act.Id]; exists {
        book.Link = act.Payload.Link
        book.Title = act.Payload.Title
        books[act.Id] = book

        status = http.StatusOK
        bookResult = []bookResource{books[act.Id]}
    }

    // Return status and updated resource.
    act.RetChan <- response{
        StatusCode: status,
        Books:      bookResult,
    }

}

func actOnPOST(books map[string]bookResource, act Action, newID string) {
    // Add the new book to 'books'.
    books[newID] = bookResource{
        Id:    newID,
        Link:  act.Payload.Link,
        Title: act.Payload.Title,
    }

    act.RetChan <- response{
        StatusCode: http.StatusCreated,
        Books:      []bookResource{books[newID]},
    }
}
```

books-handler/handler.go

The `handler.go` source file consists of all logic required to work with and handle book requests. Note that apart from consisting the logic for handling HTTP requests, it also deals with maintaining the state of books on the server:

```
// restServer/books-handler/handler.go

package booksHandler

import (
    "encoding/json"
    "fmt"
    "io/ioutil"
    "log"
```

```
        "net/http"
)

// StartBooksManager starts a goroutine that changes the state of books
(map).
// Primary reason to use a goroutine instead of directly manipulating the
books map is to ensure
// that we do not have multiple requests changing books' state
simultaneously.
func StartBooksManager(books map[string]bookResource, actionCh <-chan
Action) {
    newID := len(books)
    for {
        select {
        case act := <-actionCh:
            switch act.Type {
            case "GET":
                actOnGET(books, act)
            case "POST":
                newID++
                newBookID := fmt.Sprintf("%d", newID)
                actOnPOST(books, act, newBookID)
            case "PUT":
                actOnPUT(books, act)
            case "DELETE":
                actOnDELETE(books, act)
            }
        }
    }
}

/* BookHandler is responsible for ensuring that we process only the valid
HTTP Requests.

 * GET -> id: Any

 * POST -> id: No
 *      -> payload: Required

 * PUT -> id: Any
 *      -> payload: Required

 * DELETE -> id: Any
*/
func BookHandler(w http.ResponseWriter, r *http.Request, id string, method
string, actionCh chan<- Action) {

    // Ensure that id is set only for valid requests
```

```go
    isGet := method == "GET"
    idIsSetForPost := method == "POST" && id != ""
    isPutOrPost := method == "PUT" || method == "POST"
    idIsSetForDelPut := (method == "DELETE" || method == "PUT") && id !=
""

    if !isGet && !(idIsSetForPost || idIsSetForDelPut || isPutOrPost) {
        writeError(w, http.StatusMethodNotAllowed)
        return
    }

    respCh := make(chan response)
    act := Action{
        Id:      id,
        Type:    method,
        RetChan: respCh,
    }

    // PUT & POST require a properly formed JSON payload
    if isPutOrPost {
        var reqPayload requestPayload
        body, _ := ioutil.ReadAll(r.Body)
        defer r.Body.Close()

        if err := json.Unmarshal(body, &reqPayload); err != nil {
            writeError(w, http.StatusBadRequest)
            return
        }

        act.Payload = reqPayload
    }

    // We have all the data required to process the Request.
    // Time to update the state of books.
    actionCh <- act

    // Wait for respCh to return data after updating the state of books.
    // For all successful Actions, the HTTP status code will either be 200
or 201.
    // Any other status code means that there was an issue with the
request.
    var resp response
    if resp = <-respCh; resp.StatusCode > http.StatusCreated {
        writeError(w, resp.StatusCode)
        return
    }

    // We should only log the delete resource and not send it back to user
    if method == "DELETE" {
```

```
        log.Println(fmt.Sprintf("Resource ID %s deleted: %+v", id,
resp.Books))
        resp = response{
            StatusCode: http.StatusOK,
            Books:      []bookResource{},
        }
    }

    writeResponse(w, resp)
}
```

 Even though we have created a REST server from scratch, this is not a complete REST server. To make writing a REST server feasible, a lot of important details have been left out. But in reality, we should use one of the existing libraries that will help us build a proper REST server.

So far so good but how do we interact with a REST server and with the server based on the code we have seen so far? Let's look at this in the next section.

How to make REST calls

Up to this point, we have used the web browser to make HTTP requests. This works for a normal HTTP server or to make simple GET Requests to a REST server. However, the browser will not be able to make other type of REST calls on our behalf.

Most web applications use JavaScript, Ajax, and other frontend technologies to interact with a REST server. However, we do not have to create a full-blown web frontend to interact with a REST server; we can make use of a few tools and also write programs to make REST calls for us.

cURL

cURL is a free command-line tool used to interact over a computer network. It can be used to communicate over multiple protocols including HTTP, HTTPS, FTP, SCP, and so on. Let's make REST calls to the server created in the previous section. To improve readability, we can make use of the jq library.

GET

Let's now look at cURL commands to make HTTP requests. Depending on the state of your server, the output on making the GET Request might be different:

```
$ # List all books on server
$ # Note that we use '-L' flag while using cURL.
$ # This takes care of any http redirections that might be required.
$ curl -L localhost:8080/api/books | jq  # GET CALL
  % Total     % Received % Xferd  Average Speed   Time    Time     Time
Current
                                   Dload  Upload   Total   Spent    Left
Speed
100    46  100    46    0     0   9721      0 --:--:-- --:--:-- --:--:--
11500
100   311  100   311    0     0  59589      0 --:--:-- --:--:-- --:--:--
59589
[
  {
    "id": "3",
    "title": "Book-3",
    "link": "http://link-to-book3.com"
  },
  {
    "id": "4",
    "title": "Book-4",
    "link": "http://link-to-book4.com"
  },
  {
    "id": "5",
    "title": "Book-5",
    "link": "http://link-to-book5.com"
  },
  {
    "id": "1",
    "title": "Book-1",
    "link": "http://link-to-book1.com"
  },
  {
    "id": "2",
    "title": "Book-2",
    "link": "http://link-to-book2.com"
  }
]

$ curl localhost:8080/api/books/3 | jq  # GET a single resource.
  % Total     % Received % Xferd  Average Speed   Time    Time     Time
```

```
Current
                                       Dload  Upload   Total   Spent    Left
Speed
100    61  100    61    0     0  13255       0 --:--:-- --:--:-- --:--:--
15250
{
  "id": "3",
  "title": "Book-3",
  "link": "http://link-to-book3.com"
}
```

DELETE

Assuming that we have a book with the id `"2"`, we can delete it using cURL, as follows:

```
$ # We can make other method calls by providing -X flag with method name in
caps.
$ curl -LX DELETE localhost:8080/api/books/2 | jq  # DELETE a resource.
  % Total    % Received % Xferd  Average Speed   Time    Time     Time
Current
                                       Dload  Upload   Total   Spent    Left
Speed
100     2  100     2    0     0   337       0 --:--:-- --:--:-- --:--:--
400
[]
$ curl -L localhost:8080/api/books | jq # GET all books after resource
deletion.
  % Total    % Received % Xferd  Average Speed   Time    Time     Time
Current
                                       Dload  Upload   Total   Spent    Left
Speed
100    46  100    46    0     0  21465       0 --:--:-- --:--:-- --:--:--
46000
100   249  100   249    0     0  91008       0 --:--:-- --:--:-- --:--:--
91008
[
  {
    "id": "5",
    "title": "Book-5",
    "link": "http://link-to-book5.com"
  },
  {
    "id": "1",
    "title": "Book-1",
    "link": "http://link-to-book1.com"
  },
```

```
  {
    "id": "3",
    "title": "Book-3",
    "link": "http://link-to-book3.com"
  },
  {
    "id": "4",
    "title": "Book-4",
    "link": "http://link-to-book4.com"
  }
]
```

PUT

Let's update an existing book resource with the id "4":

```
$ # We can use -d flag to provide payload in a Request
$ curl -H "Content-Type: application/json" -LX PUT -d '{"title": "New Book
Title", "link": "New Link"}' localhost:8080/api/books/4 | jq
   % Total        % Received % Xferd  Average Speed   Time    Time     Time
Current
                                      Dload  Upload   Total   Spent    Left
Speed
100    100  100     53  100     47  13289  11785 --:--:-- --:--:-- --:--:--
17666
{
  "id": "4",
  "title": "New Book Title",
  "link": "New Link"
}
$ curl -L localhost:8080/api/books | jq # GET all books after updating a
resource
   % Total        % Received % Xferd  Average Speed   Time    Time     Time
Current
                                      Dload  Upload   Total   Spent    Left
Speed
100     46  100     46    0       0   9886      0 --:--:-- --:--:-- --:--:--
11500
100    241  100    241    0       0  47024      0 --:--:-- --:--:-- --:--:--
47024
[
  {
    "id": "1",
    "title": "Book-1",
    "link": "http://link-to-book1.com"
  },
```

```
{
  "id": "3",
  "title": "Book-3",
  "link": "http://link-to-book3.com"
},
{
  "id": "4",
  "title": "New Book Title",
  "link": "New Link"
},
{
  "id": "5",
  "title": "Book-5",
  "link": "http://link-to-book5.com"
}
]
```

POST

Now that we know how to send payload to a server using cURL, let's create a new book resource item:

```
$ curl -H "Content-Type: application/json" -LX POST -d '{"title":"Ultra New
Book", "link": "Ultra New Link"}' localhost:8080/api/books/ | jq # POST
ie., create a new resource.
```

% Total		% Received	% Xferd	Average Speed		Time	Time	Time
Current								
				Dload	Upload	Total	Spent	Left
Speed								
100	111	100	59	100	52	99k	89655	--:--:-- --:--:-- --:--:--
59000								

```
{
  "id": "6",
  "title": "Ultra New Book",
  "link": "Ultra New Link"
}
```

% Total		% Received	% Xferd	Average Speed		Time	Time	Time
Current								
				Dload	Upload	Total	Spent	Left
Speed								
100	46	100	46	0	0	8234	0	--:--:-- --:--:-- --:--:--
9200								
100	301	100	301	0	0	46414	0	--:--:-- --:--:-- --:--:--
46414								

```
[
  {
```

```
    "id": "4",
    "title": "New Book Title",
    "link": "New Link"
  },
  {
    "id": "5",
    "title": "Book-5",
    "link": "http://link-to-book5.com"
  },
  {
    "id": "1",
    "title": "Book-1",
    "link": "http://link-to-book1.com"
  },
  {
    "id": "6",
    "title": "Ultra New Book",
    "link": "Ultra New Link"
  },
  {
    "id": "3",
    "title": "Book-3",
    "link": "http://link-to-book3.com"
  }
]
```

Here are the commands for quick reference:

- `curl -L localhost:8080/api/books | jq # GET CALL`
- `curl localhost:8080/api/books/3 | jq # GET a single resource.`
- `curl -LX DELETE localhost:8080/api/books/2 | jq # DELETE a resource.`
- `curl -H "Content-Type: application/json" -LX PUT -d '{"title": "New Book Title", "link": "New Link"}' localhost:8080/api/books/4 | jq`
- `curl -H "Content-Type: application/json" -LX POST -d '{"title":"Ultra New Book", "link": "Ultra New Link"}' localhost:8080/api/books/ | jq # POST ie., create a new resource.`

And the following is the server's console output:

```
$ go run main.go
2017/10/09 21:07:50 map[5:{Id:5 Title:Book-5 Link:http://link-to-book5.com}
1:{Id:1 Title:Book-1 Link:http://link-to-book1.com} 2:{Id:2 Title:Book-2
Link:http://link-to-book2.com} 3:{Id:3 Title:Book-3
Link:http://link-to-book3.com} 4:{Id:4 Title:Book-4
Link:http://link-to-book4.com}]
2017/10/09 21:07:50 Starting server at port 8080...
2017/10/09 21:07:56 Received request [GET] for path: [/api/books/]
2017/10/09 21:07:56 ID is
2017/10/09 21:09:18 Received request [GET] for path: [/api/books/3]
2017/10/09 21:09:18 ID is   3
2017/10/09 21:11:38 Received request [DELETE] for path: [/api/books/2]
2017/10/09 21:11:38 ID is   2
2017/10/09 21:11:38 Resource ID 2 deleted: [{Id:2 Title:Book-2
Link:http://link-to-book2.com}]
2017/10/09 21:12:16 Received request [GET] for path: [/api/books/]
2017/10/09 21:12:16 ID is
2017/10/09 21:15:22 Received request [PUT] for path: [/api/books/4]
2017/10/09 21:15:22 ID is   4
2017/10/09 21:16:01 Received request [GET] for path: [/api/books/]
2017/10/09 21:16:01 ID is
2017/10/09 21:17:07 Received request [POST] for path: [/api/books/]
2017/10/09 21:17:07 ID is
2017/10/09 21:17:36 Received request [GET] for path: [/api/books/]
2017/10/09 21:17:36 ID is
```

 An important thing to keep in mind is that even though we use redirection flag -L, for POST requests the body will not be sent. We need to make sure that we are sending it to finally resolved endpoint.

This should give us the basic idea of how to use a REST client.

Postman

Let's now look at a GUI-based tool that can be used to make REST calls called **Postman** (https://www.getpostman.com/). For the sake of brevity, we shall look at a GET and a POST call.

The following screenshot illustrates how to make a GET request using Postman. Note how Postman allows us to view the returned JSON in an easy-to-read format:

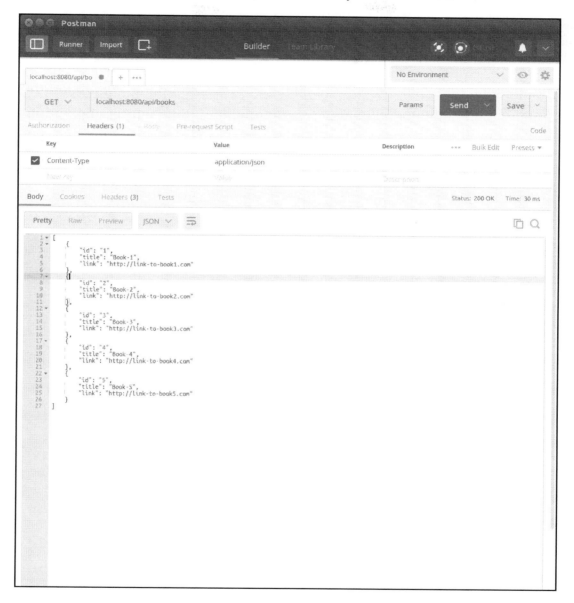

GET /api/books

The following screenshot shows how to make a POST request. Note that we could easily provide it with a JSON payload:

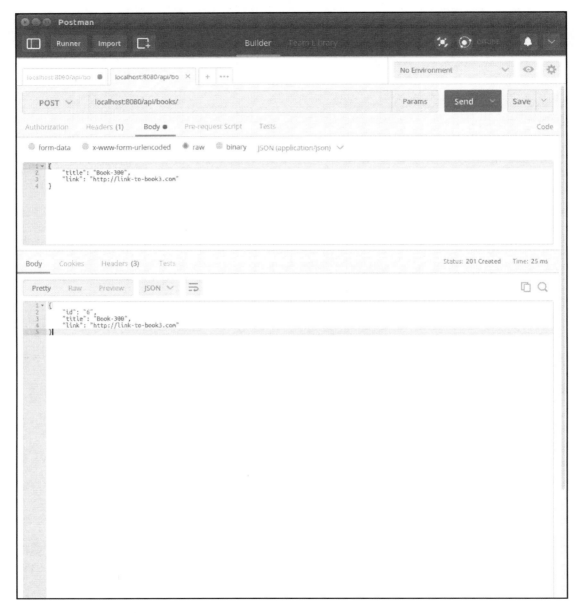

POST /api/books

Hopefully, the previous sections and these screenshots are sufficient to get an understanding of how to use Postman.

net/http

Let's look at how to send GET and POST from Go programmatically:

```go
package main

import (
    "bytes"
    "encoding/json"
    "fmt"
    "io/ioutil"
    "net/http"
)

type bookResource struct {
    Id    string 'json:"id"'
    Title string 'json:"title"'
    Link  string 'json:"link"'
}

func main() {
    // GET
    fmt.Println("Making GET call.")
    // It is possible that we might have error while making an HTTP request
    // due to too many redirects or HTTP protocol error. We should check
for this eventuality.
    resp, err := http.Get("http://localhost:8080/api/books")
    if err != nil {
        fmt.Println("Error while making GET call.", err)
        return
    }

    fmt.Printf("%+v\n\n", resp)

    // The response body is a data stream from the server we got the
response back from.
    // This data stream is not in a useable format yet.
    // We need to read it from the server and convert it into a byte
stream.
    body, _ := ioutil.ReadAll(resp.Body)
    defer resp.Body.Close()

    var books []bookResource
```

```
json.Unmarshal(body, &books)

fmt.Println(books)
fmt.Println("\n")

// POST
payload, _ := json.Marshal(bookResource{
    Title: "New Book",
    Link:  "http://new-book.com",
})

fmt.Println("Making POST call.")
resp, err = http.Post(
    "http://localhost:8080/api/books/",
    "application/json",
    bytes.NewBuffer(payload),
)
if err != nil {
    fmt.Println(err)
}

fmt.Printf("%+v\n\n", resp)

body, _ = ioutil.ReadAll(resp.Body)
defer resp.Body.Close()

var book bookResource
json.Unmarshal(body, &book)

fmt.Println(book)

fmt.Println("\n")
}
```

The following is the console output from running the program:

```
$ go run main.go

Making GET call.
&{Status:200 OK StatusCode:200 Proto:HTTP/1.1 ProtoMajor:1 ProtoMinor:1
Header:map[Content-Type:[application/json] Date:[Mon, 09 Oct 2017 20:07:43
GMT] Content-Length:[488]] Body:0xc4200f0040 ContentLength:488
TransferEncoding:[] Close:false Uncompressed:false Trailer:map[]
Request:0xc42000a900 TLS:<nil>}

[{2 Book-2 http://link-to-book2.com} {3 Book-3 http://link-to-book3.com} {4
Book-4 http://link-to-book4.com} {5 Book-5 http://link-to-book5.com} {6 New
Book http://new-book.com} {7 New Book http://new-book.com} {8 New Book
```

```
http://new-book.com} {1 Book-1 http://link-to-book1.com}]


Making POST call.
&{Status:201 Created StatusCode:201 Proto:HTTP/1.1 ProtoMajor:1
ProtoMinor:1 Header:map[Content-Type:[application/json] Date:[Mon, 09 Oct
2017 20:07:43 GMT] Content-Length:[58]] Body:0xc4200f0140 ContentLength:58
TransferEncoding:[] Close:false Uncompressed:false Trailer:map[]
Request:0xc4200fc100 TLS:<nil>}


{9 New Book http://new-book.com}
```

Further details regarding the net/http library can be found at
https://golang.org/pkg/net/http/.

Summary

In this chapter, we discussed the brief history of HTTP and sessions. Next, we looked at the problems REST protocols were designed to solve and how they came into prominence. Then, we developed a deep understanding of what a REST protocol is, how to design an application based around it, how to build a REST server based on our design, and finally we looked at different ways to interact with a REST server using cURL, Postman, and Go programs. You're free to use whichever you want to interact with a REST server. However, for the remainder of the book, we will see interactions with REST servers using cURL.

Now that we have discussed all the important topics that are fundamental to develop distributed and web-oriented applications. In the next chapter, Chapter 5, *Introducing Goophr* we can start discussing what a distributed document indexer is on a conceptual level and how to design it, plan for data communication, and so on.

5
Introducing Goophr

Now that we have a solid understanding about goroutines, channels, REST, and some of the tools for developing Go applications, let's use this knowledge to build a distributed web application. The purpose of this application will be to index and search documents. In this chapter, we will lay down the design of how such an application will be structured, and we will also look at a few remaining topics and tools that we will be using in our project.

This chapter can be broadly classified into two sections:

- Design overview
- Project structure

What is Goophr?

We will build an application to index and search documents. This is a feature that we use every time we access the internet using one of the search portals such as Google, Bing, or DuckDuckGo. This is also a feature which some sites provide with the help of a search engine.

We will build a search engine application in the next few chapters by drawing inspiration from existing technologies such as Google, the Solr search engine, and goroutines. The name of our application is a play on these three technologies.

Imagine searching for a phrase on any search portal; on submitting our query we get a list of links with snippets of text containing terms from our search phrase. Many times the first few links tend to be the relevant web page or document that we were looking for. How is it possible to get the list of the most relevant documents? The way in which Google or other search engines achieve this is quite complicated; they have a large team of Computer Scientists constantly fine-tuning the search engine.

We will not be aiming to build anything as complicated as that. By having a humble and practical goal, we can create a minimal yet usable search engine. However, first let's define the purpose and criteria for our application.

Design overview

Now that we have briefly described the application we want to build and the reason for building it, let's look at the list of features we want to implement as part of the search engine:

- It should accept links to documents provided in the POST request and download them
- It should process and index the downloaded documents
- It should handle search queries and respond with a list of documents with snippets containing the search terms
- The returned list of documents should be in the order of greater occurrence of search terms in the document

Though we listed four functionalities, we can club the application into two main components:

- **Goophr Concierge**: This is the component responsible for indexing and returning the list of documents for search queries
- **Goophr Librarian**: This is the component responsible for handling user interaction and interacting with the first component

The two components will run as two REST servers and all interactions will follow the REST protocol. So let's define API definitions for our components! In Chapter 4, *The RESTful Web*, you noticed that the approach we used to define various API endpoints and data definition for communicating via REST protocol was pretty verbose and cumbersome. Wouldn't it be better if we had a formal way to write API definitions? The good news is that with the prevalence of REST protocol, there are many solutions, and one of these solutions is the most widely used industry standard—OpenAPI format.

OpenAPI specification

OpenAPI lets us define RESTful APIs in a standardized manner, and they can be defined without being tied down to any particular programming language or framework being used. This provides us with a powerful abstraction to define an API that can have the initial implementation of the RESTful server in Java or Python; also we can port the codebase to Go, with little to no change in the behavior of the service.

Let's list the general structure of an OpenAPI specification and use it to redefine the Books API described in Chapter 4, *The RESTful Web*.

If we look at the Books API title, we can define the following elements to describe the API:

- The URL to our server
- The basic information about the intent of the API
- The paths available in our API
- The methods available per each of the paths in the API
- The possible description and example payloads for the requests and responses
- The schema of the requests and responses payloads

With these points in mind, let's look at the OpenAPI specification for Books API:

```yaml
# openapi/books.yaml

openapi: 3.0.0
servers:
  - url: /api
info:
  title: Books API
  version: '1.0'
  description: ;
    API responsible for adding, reading and updating list of books.
paths:
  /books:
    get:
      description: |
        Get list of all books
      responses:
        '200':
          description: |
            Request successfully returned list of all books
          content:
            application/json:
              schema:
```

```
              $ref: '#/components/schemas/response'
/books/{id}:
  get:
    description: |
      Get a particular books with ID 'id'
    responses:
      '200':
        description: |
          Request was successfully completed.
        content:
          application/json:
            schema:
              $ref: '#/components/schemas/document'
    parameters:
      - in: query
        name: id
        schema:
          type: integer
        description: Book ID of the book to get.
  post:
    description: |
      Get a particular books with ID 'id'
    responses:
      '200':
        description: |
          Request was successfully completed.
        content:
          application/json:
            schema:
              $ref: '#/components/schemas/payload'
    requestBody:
      content:
        application/json:
          schema:
            $ref: '#/components/schemas/document'
  put:
    description: |
      Update the data of a Book with ID 'id' with the payload sent in the
request body.
    responses:
      '200':
        description: |
          Request was successfully completed.
        content:
          application/json:
            schema:
              $ref: '#/components/schemas/payload'
    requestBody:
```

```
      content:
        application/json:
          schema:
            $ref: '#/components/schemas/document'
    delete:
      description: |
        Get a particular books with ID 'id'
      responses:
        '200':
          description: |
            Request was successfully completed.
      parameters:
        - in: query
          name: id
          schema:
            type: integer
          description: Book ID of the book to get.
components:
  schemas:
    response:
      type: array
      items:
        $ref: '#/components/schemas/document'
    document:
      type: object
      required:
        - title
        - link
      properties:
        id:
          type: integer
          description: Book ID
        title:
          type: string
          description: Title of the book
        link:
          type: string
          description: Link to the book
    payload:
      type: object
      required:
        - title
        - link
      properties:
        title:
          type: string
          description: Title of the book
        link:
```

```
          type: string
          description: Link to the book
```

Goophr Concierge API definition

Goophr Concierge is the user-facing component, and it has two responsibilities—to index new documents and to return query results. Informally, we can define the API as follows:

- /api/feeder: This is the API endpoint to upload documents by user
    - The POST request adds new documents if the payload is complete and correct
- /api/query: The user searches for phrases or terms that are queried against this API endpoint
    - The POST request contains payload with search terms, and a list of documents will be returned

This simple API description is for our understanding. Now let's look at how this would be formulated using the OpenAPI specification:

```
# openapi/concierge.yaml

openapi: 3.0.0

servers:
  - url: /api
info:
  title: Goophr Concierge API
  version: '1.0'
  description: >
    API responsible for responding to user input and communicating with
Goophr
    Librarian.
paths:
  /feeder:
    post:
      description: |
        Register new document to be indexed.
      responses:
        '200':
          description: |
            Request was successfully completed.
          content:
            application/json:
              schema:
```

```
                $ref: '#/components/schemas/response'
        '400':
          description: >
            Request was not processed because payload was incomplete or
            incorrect.
          content:
            application/json:
              schema:
                $ref: '#/components/schemas/response'
      requestBody:
        content:
          application/json:
            schema:
              $ref: '#/components/schemas/document'
        required: true
  /query:
    post:
      description: |
        Search query
      responses:
        '200':
          description: |
            Response consists of links to document
          content:
            application/json:
              schema:
                type: array
                items:
                  $ref: '#/components/schemas/document'
      requestBody:
        content:
          application/json:
            schema:
              type: array
              items:
                type: string
        required: true
components:
  schemas:
    response:
      type: object
      properties:
        code:
          type: integer
          description: Status code to send in response
        msg:
          type: string
          description: Message to send in response
```

```
document:
  type: object
  required:
    - title
    - link
  properties:
    title:
      type: string
      description: Title of the document
    link:
      type: string
      description: Link to the document
```

With the help of the API description, the preceding OpenAPI definition should be self-explanatory. Details regarding the OpenAPI specification can be found at `https://swagger.io/specification/`. We can use tools provided by Swagger (`https://editor.swagger.io/`) to get a better visual representation of our API definition.

The following is the screenshot of the Goophr Concierge OpenAPI as viewed in Swagger Editor:

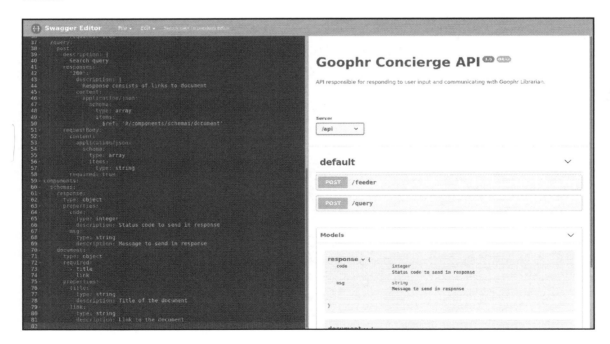

Viewing OpenAPI on Swagger Editor

Goophr Librarian API definition

Goophr Librarian is the actual maintainer of the index for a set of documents, and its responsibilities are to add terms to the index and to return query results for the search terms based on the terms available in the index.

Informally, we can define the API as follows:

- /api/index: Goophr Concierge calls this API endpoint to add terms to the actual index
    - The POST request adds terms to index
- /api/query: Goophr Concierge calls this endpoint to query search terms submitted by the user
    - The POST request returns results for search terms

The following is the OpenAPI definition for Goophr Librarian:

```yaml
# openapi/librarian.yaml

openapi: 3.0.0
servers:
  - url: /api
info:
  title: Goophr Librarian API
  version: '1.0'
  description: |
    API responsible for indexing & communicating with Goophr Concierge.
paths:
  /index:
    post:
      description: |
        Add terms to index.
      responses:
        '200':
          description: |
            Terms were successfully added to the index.
        '400':
          description: >
            Request was not processed because payload was incomplete or
            incorrect.
          content:
            application/json:
              schema:
                $ref: '#/components/schemas/error'
      requestBody:
```

```
            content:
              application/json:
                schema:
                  $ref: '#/components/schemas/terms'
            description: |
              List of terms to be added to the index.
            required: true
  /query:
    post:
      description: |
        Search for all terms in the payload.
      responses:
        '200':
          description: |
            Returns a list of all the terms along with their frequency,
            documents the terms appear in and link to the said documents.
          content:
            application/json:
              schema:
                $ref: '#/components/schemas/results'
        '400':
          description: >
            Request was not processed because payload was incomplete or
            incorrect.
          content:
            application/json:
              schema:
                $ref: '#/components/schemas/error'
      parameters: []
components:
  schemas:
    error:
      type: object
      properties:
        msg:
          type: string
    term:
      type: object
      required:
        - title
        - token
        - doc_id
        - line_index
        - token_index
      properties:
        title:
          description: |
            Title of the document to which the term belongs.
```

```
        type: string
    token:
      description: |
        The term to be added to the index.
      type: string
    doc_id:
      description: |
        The unique hash for each document.
      type: string
    line_index:
      description: |
        Line index at which the term occurs in the document.
      type: integer
    token_index:
      description: |
        Position of the term in the document.
      type: integer
terms:
  type: object
  properties:
    code:
      type: integer
    data:
      type: array
      items:
        $ref: '#/components/schemas/term'
results:
  type: object
  properties:
    count:
      type: integer
    data:
      type: array
      items:
        $ref: '#/components/schemas/result'
result:
  type: object
  properties:
    doc_id:
      type: string
    score:
      type: integer
```

The two API specifications describe how the two components will interact with each other and also the user. However, this is not the complete picture because even though we have shown only two API definitions, the actual implementation will have three instances of Librarian!

The user interacts with Goophr by interacting with Concierge via `/api/feeder` and `/api/query`. Concierge can further interact with the three librarian instances via `/api/index` and `/api/query`. The figure below shows what the application will look like in broad terms:

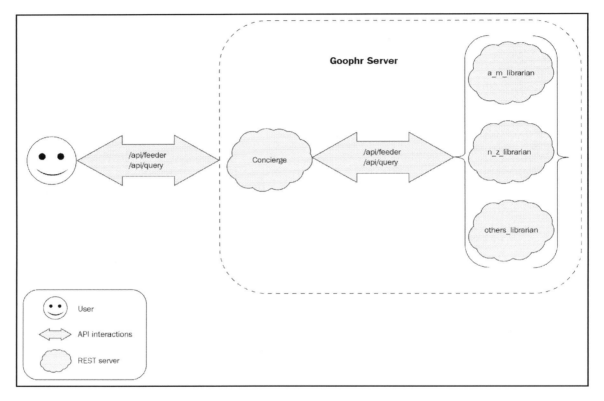

The design of the Goophr application

Consider when we need to build a real web application that will be used by multiple users; in this case, we'll want to have multiple instances of our services running so that they can serve all the users simultaneously. We might also have split our application into multiple APIs, and we need to have a good understanding on how to design our system to handle such distributed workload. So, in order to understand how to deal with such a system, we will work with three instances of Librarian.

Project structure

As per the previous diagram, we have designed our application to consist of one instance of Goophr Concierge and three instances of Goophr Librarian. In order to keep our code manageable, we will split the source code into two main entities and a docker-compose file at the root level:

- Concierge
- Librarian
- docker-compose.yaml

In Chapter 1, *Developer Environment for Go*, we discussed how to create and run docker images. The docker run ... works great for single images, but it might get complicated when we want to create a network of docker images that interact with one another. In order to keep the setup simple, we will make use of docker-compose (https://docs.docker.com/compose/overview/). In a nutshell, docker-compose requires a **YAML (Yet Another Markup Language)** file with specifics such as what to name the running docker images, what ports to run them on, and which Dockerfile to use to build these docker images.

The following is the docker-compose.yaml file we will be using in our project:

```
version: '3'

services:
  concierge:
    build: concierge/.
    ports:
      - "6060:9000"
  a_m_librarian:
    build: librarian/.
    ports:
      - "7070:9000"
  n_z_librarian:
    build: librarian/.
    ports:
      - "8080:9000"
  others_librarian:
    build: librarian/.
    ports:
      - "9090:9000"
```

Note that `a_m_librarian`, `n_z_librarian`, and `others_librarian` are built from the same docker image defined by `librarian/Dockerfile`. This makes our life easier than using raw `docker` commands to start and configure multiple instances.

Here is the project structure that we will be starting with:

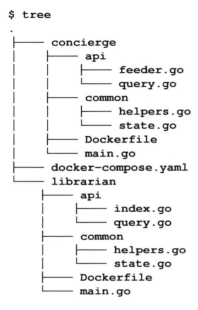

```
$ tree
.
├── concierge
│   ├── api
│   │   ├── feeder.go
│   │   └── query.go
│   ├── common
│   │   ├── helpers.go
│   │   └── state.go
│   ├── Dockerfile
│   └── main.go
├── docker-compose.yaml
└── librarian
    ├── api
    │   ├── index.go
    │   └── query.go
    ├── common
    │   ├── helpers.go
    │   └── state.go
    ├── Dockerfile
    └── main.go
```

Even though we have an elaborate structure set up, for now, the only files that have any useful code are `concierge/main.go`, `concierge/Dockerfile`, `librarian/main.go`, and `librarian/Dockerfile` (for convenience, from here on, we will denote the files using shorthand notation `{concierge,librarian}/{main.go,Dockerfile}`. This notation is inspired from Bash.)

Let's take a look at `main.go` and `Dockerfile`. These two files will be almost identical for both components. For brevity, we will show each of the two types of the files once, and show where the differences lie.

Let's start with `main.go`:

```go
// {concierge,librarian}/main.go
package main

import "fmt"

func main() {
```

```
    fmt.Println("Hello from Concierge!")   // Or, Hello from Librarian!
}
```

Now let's look at `Dockerfile`:

```
# {concierge,librarian}/Dockerfile
FROM golang:1.9.1

# In case of librarian, '/concierge' will be replaced with '/librarian'

ADD . /go/src/github.com/last-ent/distributed-go/chapter5/goophr/concierge

WORKDIR /go/src/github.com/last-ent/distributed-
go/chapter5/goophr/concierge

RUN go install github.com/last-ent/distributed-go/chapter5/goophr/concierge

ENTRYPOINT /go/bin/concierge

EXPOSE 9000
```

If we run the complete codebase, we should see an output similar to the following:

```
$ docker-compose up --build
# ...
Creating goophr_a_m_librarian_1 ...
Creating goophr_concierge_1 ...
Creating goophr_m_z_librarian_1 ...
Creating goophr_others_librarian_1 ...
Creating goophr_a_m_librarian_1
Creating goophr_m_z_librarian_1
Creating goophr_others_librarian_1
Creating goophr_others_librarian_1 ... done
Attaching to goophr_a_m_librarian_1, goophr_m_z_librarian_1,
goophr_concierge_1, goophr_others_librarian_1
a_m_librarian_1      | Hello from Librarian!
m_z_librarian_1      | Hello from Librarian!
others_librarian_1   | Hello from Librarian!
concierge_1          | Hello from Concierge!
goophr_a_m_librarian_1 exited with code 0
goophr_m_z_librarian_1 exited with code 0
goophr_concierge_1 exited with code 0
goophr_others_librarian_1 exited with code 0
```

Summary

In this chapter, we started by describing the application that we will be building in the next three chapters. Then we split the application into two major components—Goophr Concierge and Goophr Librarian. Next we looked at the project structure that we will be using for our application. We also discussed OpenAPI, the industry standard for describing REST APIs, and used it to define our APIs for Concierge and Librarian. Finally, we looked at how to run our distributed application using `docker-compose`.

In the next chapter, we will look at Goophr Concierge, which will interact with users to upload documents, and respond to the search queries from users.

6
Goophr Concierge

In the previous chapter, Chapter 5, *Introducing Goophr*, we split our application into two components: Concierge and Librarian. In this chapter, we shall look at the design and implementation of Concierge. The following are the major sections in this chapter:

- A deeper look at document feeder and query handler APIs
- Diagrams explaining the architecture and logical flow of Concierge
- Tests for Concierge

Revisiting the API definition

Let's have another look at the API definition for Concierge, and discuss what the definition conveys regarding the expected behavior by the API and application:

```
# openapi/concierge.yaml

openapi: 3.0.0
servers:
  - url: /api
info:
  title: Goophr Concierge API
  version: '1.0'
  description: >
    API responsible for responding to user input and communicating with Goophr
    Librarian.
paths:
  /feeder:
    post:
      description: |
```

```
            Register new document to be indexed.
        responses:
          '200':
            description: |
              Request was successfully completed.
            content:
              application/json:
                schema:
                  $ref: '#/components/schemas/response'
          '400':
            description: >
              Request was not processed because payload was incomplete or
incorrect.
            content:
              application/json:
                schema:
                  $ref: '#/components/schemas/response'
        requestBody:
          content:
            application/json:
              schema:
                $ref: '#/components/schemas/document'
          required: true
  /query:
    post:
      description: |
        Search query
      responses:
        '200':
          description: |
            Response consists of links to document
          content:
            application/json:
              schema:
                type: array
                items:
                  $ref: '#/components/schemas/document'
      requestBody:
        content:
          application/json:
            schema:
              type: array
              items:
                type: string
        required: true
components:
  schemas:
    response:
```

```
          type: object
          properties:
            code:
              type: integer
              description: Status code to send in response
            msg:
              type: string
              description: Message to send in response
        document:
          type: object
          required:
            - title
            - link
          properties:
            title:
              type: string
              description: Title of the document
            link:
              type: string
              description: Link to the document
```

Based on the API definition, we can state the following:

- All communication to and from Concierge is using the JSON format
- Two endpoints for Concierge are /api/feeder and /api/query
  - /api/feeder: This uses the POST method to add new documents
  - /api/query: This uses the POST method to receive search query terms and returns a list of documents related to the search term

Now let's look at each of the endpoints in detail.

Document feeder – the REST API endpoint

The main aim of /api/feeder is to receive documents to be indexed, process them, and forward the processed data to Librarian to be added to the index. This means we need to accurately process the document. But what do we mean by "processing a document?"

It can be defined as the following set of consecutive tasks:

1. We rely on the payload to provide us with a title and link to the document. We download the linked document and use it in our index.

2. The document can be thought of as one big blob of text, and it is possible that we might have multiple documents with the same title. We need to be able to identify each document uniquely and also be able to easily retrieve them.

3. The result of a search query expects the provided words to be present in the document. This means we need to extract all words from a document and also keep track of where a word occurs within a document.

4. Would it make sense to differentiate between "HELLO", "hello", and "HELLO!!!"? In the context of the text it occurs in, they certainly convey different meanings. However, for the index, it depends on how complex and accurate we want to make our index. For our case, we keep the implementation simple, and thus we normalize the words, that is, we treat all these variations of the word as a single unit/token. Additionally, we do not index pronouns, articles, propositions, and so on.

 For a search engine, pronouns, articles, and so on are termed as **stop words**, and it is common to ignore them in the index. The main reason is that while they provide valuable information for the user, they tend to have little to no relevance for the index.

5. Finally, we would like to add all these tokens to the index maintained by the Librarian.

In the source code for Concierge, each of the preceding tasks stated is handled by certain functions. The following is a list showing associated functions for each of the tasks:

- Task 1: `api.FeedHandler` and `api.docProcessor`
- Task 2: `api.docStore` and `api.lineStore`
- Task 3 and Task 4: `api.indexProcessor` and `common.SimplifyToken`
- Task 5: `api.indexAdder`

Query handler – the REST API endpoint

Similarly, if we consider the case of handling a search query at /api/query, we should be able to take the search terms from the payload, request results from various instances of the Librarian, process them, and then return search results back to the user in the descending order of search relevance. However, since we haven't implemented the Librarian yet, we shall discuss the implementation of this endpoint later in Chapter 8, *Deploying Goophr*, the distributed search index.

Conventions

The source code for Concierge has a lot of moving parts. Directly jumping into the code without any prior understanding might not be the best way to proceed. Instead, we shall take the tasks defined in the previous sections and present them as flow diagrams. However, first, let's have a brief look at the symbols and naming conventions we are using in the diagrams and code.

Code conventions

Following are the entities in Concierge:

- **payload (p)**: This represents the payload received to add a new document to index.
- **document (d)**: This represents all the metadata representing a unique document.
- **line (l)**: This represents all the metadata for a single line within a document.
- **token (t)**: This represents all the metadata for each token within a document.
- **Message (xMsg)**: For a given entity, **x**, it provides information to identify a unique entity and a callback channel to return the unique entity.
- **Process Channels (xProcessCh)**: For a given entity, **x**, the channel is used by **xProcessor** goroutine to consume and process the entity.
- **Stores** (or **Data Stores**): The Concierge is also responsible for storing and maintaining information regarding all the documents and lines in the system.
- **Store Channels** (xStoreCh): For a given entity, **x**, the channel is used to update the entity's store.
- **Get Channels (xGetCh** or **xGetAllCh)**: These channels are used by stores to provide a mechanism to retrieve an entity using callback channels.
- **done**: This is a special channel that will stop all running goroutines once it is closed. We should be careful to close this channel and not send a message on it, the reason being that sending a message will only signal a single goroutine to stop. Instead, if we were to close the channel, all goroutines listening on the channel will receive message to stop.

Let's look at a few examples so that we have perfect understanding of the conventions:

- **dStoreCh**: This is the channel to add new documents to Document Store
- **dGetCh**: This is the channel to get a single document from Document Store

Diagram conventions

Next, let's look at the symbols we will be using in our diagrams:

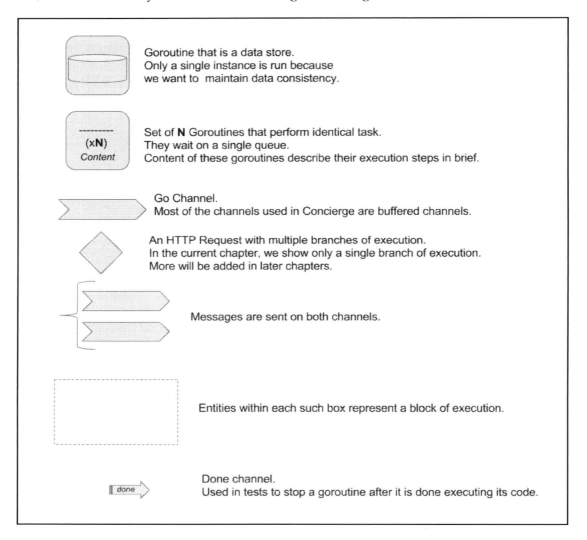

Now, let's proceed to visualize Concierge's logic with help of logical flow diagrams.

Logical flow diagrams

We can split the logic for Concierge into five major chunks. We shall address the required logic flow for each of the individual chunks, and then at the end, combine them all to get the big picture of what we are trying to achieve.

The doc processor

First and foremost, we want to accept the payload sent to endpoint and start processing the document. Let's assume that `api.FeedHandler` accepts, validates, and sends the payload on **pProcessCh**:

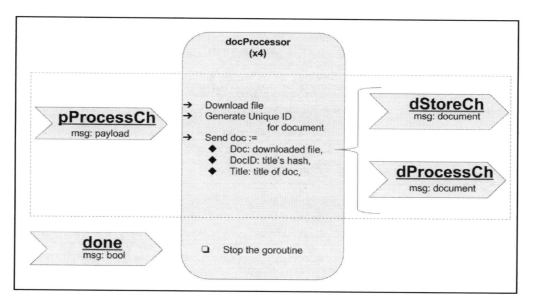

The doc store

Let's then consider **dStoreCh**, which is the channel used for adding and retrieving documents:

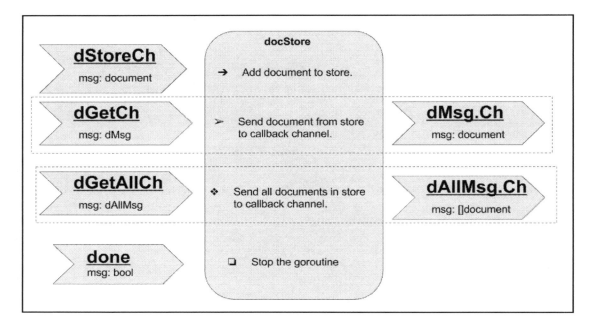

The index processor

Apart from adding to docstore, docProcessor also sends the document to indexProcessor, which is responsible for storing lines in the document and converting lines into tokens:

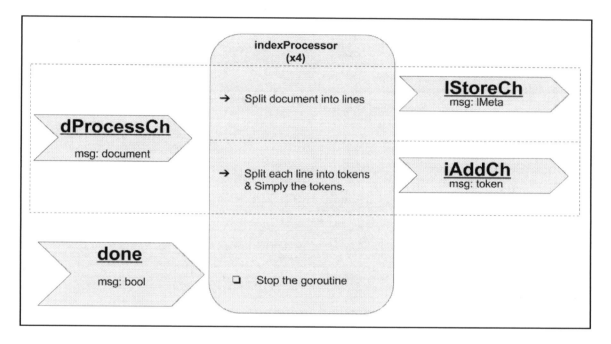

The line store

`indexProcessor` splits the document into lines, and `lineStore` is responsible for storing them and also returning them when queried:

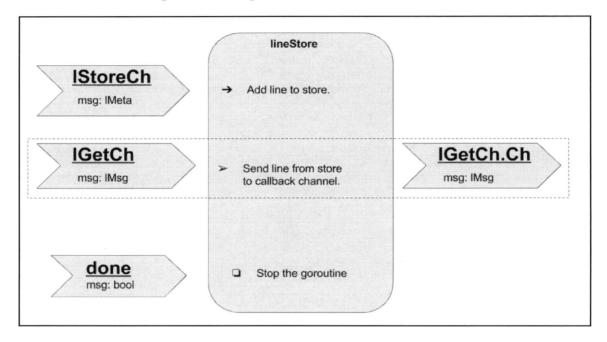

`indexProcessor` also splits the lines into tokens and adds them to `iAddCh` channel. `indexAdder` is responsible for adding these tokens to the index (Librarian).

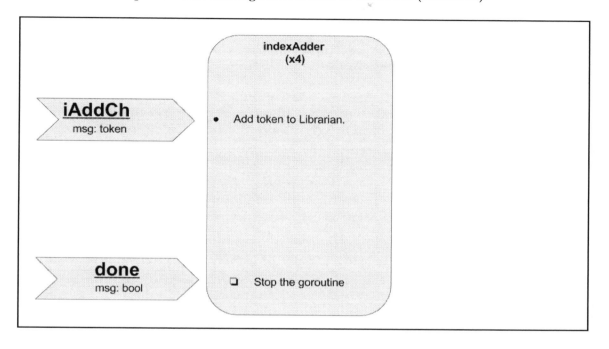

The consolidated flow diagram

Now that we have defined each of the individual chunks, you might have noticed that they flow into one another and have some components that they share among themselves. Let us consolidate all of these flow diagrams now:

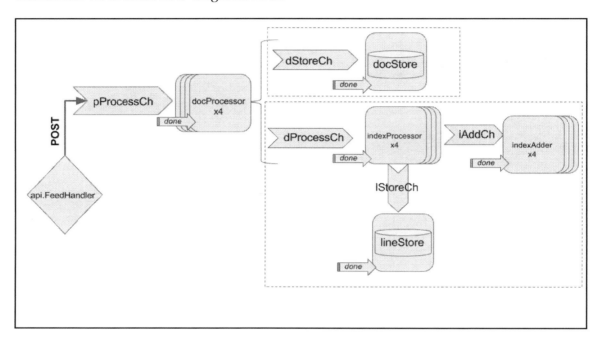

This might be a good opportunity to try and build Concierge on your own. However, please read the following three design points to have complete knowledge of the system.

Queue workers

In the consolidated flow diagram, you might have noticed that we run four instances of docProcessor, indexProcessor, and indexAdder. The reason for this is that the tasks handled by these goroutines are embarrassingly parallel, that is, they can be run in parallel without side effects. This allows us to parallelize and process the documents at a faster pace.

Single stores

In contrast, we run `docStore` and `lineStore` as single instances because we want to a maintain consistent state for these stores.

Buffered channels

For almost all the channels in our code, we will be using buffered channels with a capacity of 8. This allows us to avoid blocking the `api.FeedHandler` endpoint in case `docProcessors` are busy. Also because of queue workers and single stores, `lStoreCh` and `dStoreCh` have a capacity of 16 each.

The Concierge source code

Now that we have discussed the design of Concierge in detail, let us implement Concierge based on these design points. We will discuss the implementation of `api/query.go` and Dockerfile in *Chapter 8, Deploying Goophr*. Let's look at the project structure & source code:

```
$ tree
.
└── goophr
    └── concierge
        ├── api
        │   ├── feeder.go
        │   ├── feeder_test.go
        │   └── query.go
        ├── common
        │   ├── helpers.go
        ├── Dockerfile
        └── main.go

4 directories, 6 files
```

Now let's look at the source code for each of the files:

main.go:

```
package main

import (
    "net/http"

    "github.com/last-ent/distributed-go/chapter6/goophr/concierge/api"
```

```
        "github.com/last-ent/distributed-go/chapter6/goophr/concierge/common"
)

func main() {
    common.Log("Adding API handlers...")
    http.HandleFunc("/api/feeder", api.FeedHandler)

    common.Log("Starting feeder...")
    api.StartFeederSystem()

    common.Log("Starting Goophr Concierge server on port :8080...")
    http.ListenAndServe(":8080", nil)
}
```

common/helpers.go:

```
package common

import (
    "fmt"
    "log"
    "regexp"
    "strings"
)

// Log is used for simple logging to console.
func Log(msg string) {
    log.Println("INFO - ", msg)
}

// Warn is used to log warning messages to console.
func Warn(msg string) {
    log.Println("-------------------------")
    log.Println(fmt.Sprintf("WARN: %s", msg))
    log.Println("-------------------------")
}

var punctuations = regexp.MustCompile('^\p{P}+|\p{P}+$')

// List of stop words that we want to ignore in our index.
var stopWords = []string{
    "a", "about", "above", "after", "again", "against", "all", "am", "an",
"and", "any", "are", "aren't", "as", "at",
    "be", "because", "been", "before", "being", "below", "between", "both",
"but", "by", "can't", "cannot", "could",
    "couldn't", "did", "didn't", "do", "does", "doesn't", "doing", "don't",
"down", "during", "each", "few", "for",
    "from", "further", "had", "hadn't", "has", "hasn't", "have", "haven't",
```

```
    "having", "he", "he'd", "he'll", "he's",
        "her", "here", "here's", "hers", "herself", "him", "himself", "his",
    "how", "how's", "i", "i'd", "i'll", "i'm",
        "i've", "if", "in", "into", "is", "isn't", "it", "it's", "its",
    "itself", "let's", "me", "more", "most", "mustn't",
        "my", "myself", "no", "nor", "not", "of", "off", "on", "once", "only",
    "or", "other", "ought", "our", "ours",
        "ourselves", "out", "over", "own", "same", "shan't", "she", "she'd",
    "she'll", "she's", "should", "shouldn't",
        "so", "some", "such", "than", "that", "that's", "the", "their",
    "theirs", "them", "themselves", "then", "there",
        "there's", "these", "they", "they'd", "they'll", "they're", "they've",
    "this", "those", "through", "to", "too",
        "under", "until", "up", "very", "was", "wasn't", "we", "we'd", "we'll",
    "we're", "we've", "were", "weren't", "what",
        "what's", "when", "when's", "where", "where's", "which", "while",
    "who", "who's", "whom", "why", "why's", "with",
        "won't", "would", "wouldn't", "you", "you'd", "you'll", "you're",
    "you've", "your", "yours", "yourself", "yourselves"}

// SimplifyToken is responsible to normalizing a string token and
// also checks whether the token should be indexed or not.
func SimplifyToken(token string) (string, bool) {
    simpleToken := strings.ToLower(punctuations.ReplaceAllString(token,
""))

    for _, stopWord := range stopWords {
        if stopWord == simpleToken {
            return "", false
        }
    }

    return simpleToken, true
}
```

api/feeder.go:

```
package api

import (
    "crypto/sha1"
    "encoding/json"
    "fmt"
    "io/ioutil"
    "net/http"
    "strings"
    "time"
```

```
        "github.com/last-ent/distributed-go/chapter6/goophr/concierge/common"
)

type payload struct {
    URL   string 'json:"url"'
    Title string 'json:"title"'
}

type document struct {
    Doc   string 'json:"-"'
    Title string 'json:"title"'
    DocID string 'json:"DocID"'

}

type token struct {
    Line   string 'json:"-"'
    Token  string 'json:"token"'
    Title  string 'json:"title"'
    DocID  string 'json:"doc_id"'
    LIndex int    'json:"line_index"'
    Index  int    'json:"token_index"'
}

type dMsg struct {
    DocID string
    Ch    chan document
}

type lMsg struct {
    LIndex int
    DocID  string
    Ch     chan string
}

type lMeta struct {
    LIndex int
    DocID  string
    Line   string
}

type dAllMsg struct {
    Ch chan []document
}

// done signals all listening goroutines to stop.
var done chan bool
```

```go
// dGetCh is used to retrieve a single document from store.
var dGetCh chan dMsg

// lGetCh is used to retrieve a single line from store.
var lGetCh chan lMsg

// lStoreCh is used to put a line into store.
var lStoreCh chan lMeta

// iAddCh is used to add token to index (Librarian).
var iAddCh chan token

// dStoreCh is used to put a document into store.
var dStoreCh chan document

// dProcessCh is used to process a document and convert it to tokens.
var dProcessCh chan document

// dGetAllCh is used to retrieve all documents in store.
var dGetAllCh chan dAllMsg

// pProcessCh is used to process the /feeder's payload and start the
indexing process.
var pProcessCh chan payload

// StartFeederSystem initializes all channels and starts all goroutines.
// We are using a standard function instead of 'init()'
// because we don't want the channels & goroutines to be initialized during
testing.
// Unless explicitly required by a particular test.
func StartFeederSystem() {
    done = make(chan bool)

    dGetCh = make(chan dMsg, 8)
    dGetAllCh = make(chan dAllMsg)

    iAddCh = make(chan token, 8)
    pProcessCh = make(chan payload, 8)

    dStoreCh = make(chan document, 8)
    dProcessCh = make(chan document, 8)
    lGetCh = make(chan lMsg)
    lStoreCh = make(chan lMeta, 8)

    for i := 0; i < 4; i++ {
        go indexAdder(iAddCh, done)
        go docProcessor(pProcessCh, dStoreCh, dProcessCh, done)
        go indexProcessor(dProcessCh, lStoreCh, iAddCh, done)
```

```
        }

        go docStore(dStoreCh, dGetCh, dGetAllCh, done)
        go lineStore(lStoreCh, lGetCh, done)
    }

    // indexAdder adds token to index (Librarian).
    func indexAdder(ch chan token, done chan bool) {
        for {
            select {
            case tok := <-ch:
                fmt.Println("adding to librarian:", tok.Token)

            case <-done:
                common.Log("Exiting indexAdder.")
                return
            }
        }
    }

    // lineStore maintains a catalog of all lines for all documents being
    indexed.
    func lineStore(ch chan lMeta, callback chan lMsg, done chan bool) {
        store := map[string]string{}
        for {
            select {
            case line := <-ch:
                id := fmt.Sprintf("%s-%d", line.DocID, line.LIndex)
                store[id] = line.Line

            case ch := <-callback:
                line := ""
                id := fmt.Sprintf("%s-%d", ch.DocID, ch.LIndex)
                if l, exists := store[id]; exists {
                    line = l
                }
                ch.Ch <- line
            case <-done:
                common.Log("Exiting docStore.")
                return
            }
        }
    }

    // indexProcessor is responsible for converting a document into tokens for
    indexing.
    func indexProcessor(ch chan document, lStoreCh chan lMeta, iAddCh chan
    token, done chan bool) {
```

```
    for {
        select {
        case doc := <-ch:
            docLines := strings.Split(doc.Doc, "\n")

            lin := 0
            for _, line := range docLines {
                if strings.TrimSpace(line) == "" {
                    continue
                }

                lStoreCh <- lMeta{
                    LIndex: lin,
                    Line:   line,
                    DocID:  doc.DocID,
                }

                index := 0
                words := strings.Fields(line)
                for _, word := range words {
                    if tok, valid := common.SimplifyToken(word); valid {
                        iAddCh <- token{
                            Token: tok,
                            LIndex: lin,
                            Line:  line,
                            Index: index,
                            DocID: doc.DocID,
                            Title: doc.Title,
                        }
                        index++
                    }
                }
                lin++
            }

        case <-done:
            common.Log("Exiting indexProcessor.")
            return
        }
    }
}

// docStore maintains a catalog of all documents being indexed.
func docStore(add chan document, get chan dMsg, dGetAllCh chan dAllMsg,
done chan bool) {
    store := map[string]document{}

    for {
```

```
        select {
        case doc := <-add:
            store[doc.DocID] = doc
        case m := <-get:
            m.Ch <- store[m.DocID]
        case ch := <-dGetAllCh:
            docs := []document{}
            for _, doc := range store {
                docs = append(docs, doc)
            }
            ch.Ch <- docs
        case <-done:
            common.Log("Exiting docStore.")
            return
        }
    }
}

// docProcessor processes new document payloads.
func docProcessor(in chan payload, dStoreCh chan document, dProcessCh chan
document, done chan bool) {
    for {
        select {
        case newDoc := <-in:
            var err error
            doc := ""

            if doc, err = getFile(newDoc.URL); err != nil {
                common.Warn(err.Error())
                continue
            }

            titleID := getTitleHash(newDoc.Title)
            msg := document{
                Doc:   doc,
                DocID: titleID,
                Title: newDoc.Title,
            }

            dStoreCh <- msg
            dProcessCh <- msg
        case <-done:
            common.Log("Exiting docProcessor.")
            return
        }
    }
}
```

```go
// getTitleHash returns a new hash ID everytime it is called.
// Based on: https://gobyexample.com/sha1-hashes

func getTitleHash(title string) string {

    hash := sha1.New()
    title = strings.ToLower(title)

    str := fmt.Sprintf("%s-%s", time.Now(), title)
    hash.Write([]byte(str))

    hByte := hash.Sum(nil)

    return fmt.Sprintf("%x", hByte)
}

// getFile returns file content after retrieving it from URL.
func getFile(URL string) (string, error) {
    var res *http.Response
    var err error

    if res, err = http.Get(URL); err != nil {
        errMsg := fmt.Errorf("Unable to retrieve URL: %s.\nError: %s", URL,
err)

        return "", errMsg

    }
    if res.StatusCode > 200 {
        errMsg := fmt.Errorf("Unable to retrieve URL: %s.\nStatus Code:
%d", URL, res.StatusCode)

        return "", errMsg
    }

    body, err := ioutil.ReadAll(res.Body)
    defer res.Body.Close()

    if err != nil {
        errMsg := fmt.Errorf("Error while reading response: URL:
%s.\nError: %s", URL, res.StatusCode, err.Error())

        return "", errMsg
    }

    return string(body), nil
}
```

```go
// FeedHandler start processing the payload which contains the file to
index.
func FeedHandler(w http.ResponseWriter, r *http.Request) {
    if r.Method == "GET" {
        ch := make(chan []document)
        dGetAllCh <- dAllMsg{Ch: ch}
        docs := <-ch
        close(ch)

        if serializedPayload, err := json.Marshal(docs); err == nil {
            w.Write(serializedPayload)
        } else {
            common.Warn("Unable to serialize all docs: " + err.Error())
            w.WriteHeader(http.StatusInternalServerError)
            w.Write([]byte('{"code": 500, "msg": "Error occurred while
trying to retrieve documents."}'))
        }
        return
    } else if r.Method != "POST" {
        w.WriteHeader(http.StatusMethodNotAllowed)
        w.Write([]byte('{"code": 405, "msg": "Method Not Allowed."}'))
        return
    }

    decoder := json.NewDecoder(r.Body)
    defer r.Body.Close()

    var newDoc payload
    decoder.Decode(&newDoc)
    pProcessCh <- newDoc

    w.Write([]byte('{"code": 200, "msg": "Request is being processed."}'))
}
```

api/feeder_test.go:

```go
package api

import (
    "fmt"
    "net/http"
    "net/http/httptest"
    "testing"
)

func TestGetTitleHash(t *testing.T) {

    h1 := getTitleHash("A-Title")
```

```go
    h2 := getTitleHash("Diff Title")
    hDup := getTitleHash("A-Title")

    for _, tc := range []struct {
        name        string
        hashes      []string
        expected bool
    }{
        {"Different Titles", []string{h1, h2}, false},
        {"Duplicate Titles", []string{h1, hDup}, false},
        {"Same hashes", []string{h2, h2}, true},
    } {
        t.Run(tc.name, func(t *testing.T) {
            actual := tc.hashes[0] == tc.hashes[1]
            if actual != tc.expected {
                t.Error(actual, tc.expected, tc.hashes)
            }
        })
    }
}

func TestGetFile(t *testing.T) {
    doc := "Server returned text!"
    testServer := httptest.NewServer(http.HandlerFunc(func(w
http.ResponseWriter, r *http.Request) {
        w.Write([]byte(doc))
    }))
    defer testServer.Close()

    rDoc, err := getFile(testServer.URL)
    if err != nil {
        t.Error("Error while retrieving document", err)
    }
    if doc != rDoc {
        t.Error(doc, "!=", rDoc)
    }
}

func TestIndexProcessor(t *testing.T) {
    ch1 := make(chan document, 1)
    ch2 := make(chan lMeta, 1)
    ch3 := make(chan token, 3)
    done := make(chan bool)

    go indexProcessor(ch1, ch2, ch3, done)

    ch1 <- document{
        DocID: "a-hash",
```

```
        Title: "a-title",
        Doc:   "Golang Programming rocks!",
    }

    for i, tc := range []string{
        "golang", "programming", "rocks",
    } {
        t.Run(fmt.Sprintf("Testing if '%s' is returned. at index: %d", tc,
    i), func(t *testing.T) {
            tok := <-ch3
            if tok.Token != tc {
                t.Error(tok.Token, "!=", tc)
            }
            if tok.Index != i {
                t.Error(tok.Index, "!=", i)
            }
        })
    }
    close(done)

}
```

Running tests

In `api/feeder_test.go`, we have three main test case scenarios:

- To test if a unique hash is generated for each new document
- Testing if payload sent to the `/api/feeder` endpoint returns document content as expected
- Test to ensure the indexing of documents is working as expected

The following is the expected output after running the tests:

```
$ go test -v ./...
?       github.com/last-ent/distributed-go/chapter6/goophr/concierge
[no test files]
=== RUN   TestGetTitleHash
=== RUN   TestGetTitleHash/Different_Titles
=== RUN   TestGetTitleHash/Duplicate_Titles
=== RUN   TestGetTitleHash/Same_hashes
--- PASS: TestGetTitleHash (0.00s)
    --- PASS: TestGetTitleHash/Different_Titles (0.00s)
    --- PASS: TestGetTitleHash/Duplicate_Titles (0.00s)
    --- PASS: TestGetTitleHash/Same_hashes (0.00s)
=== RUN   TestGetFile
```

```
--- PASS: TestGetFile (0.00s)
=== RUN    TestIndexProcessor
=== RUN
TestIndexProcessor/Testing_if_'golang'_is_returned._at_index:_1
=== RUN
TestIndexProcessor/Testing_if_'programming'_is_returned._at_index:_2
=== RUN
TestIndexProcessor/Testing_if_'rocks'_is_returned._at_index:_3
--- PASS: TestIndexProcessor (0.00s)
    --- PASS:
TestIndexProcessor/Testing_if_'golang'_is_returned._at_index:_1 (0.00s)
    --- PASS:
TestIndexProcessor/Testing_if_'programming'_is_returned._at_index:_2
(0.00s)
    --- PASS:
TestIndexProcessor/Testing_if_'rocks'_is_returned._at_index:_3 (0.00s)
PASS
ok      github.com/last-ent/distributed-
go/chapter6/goophr/concierge/api        0.004s
?       github.com/last-ent/distributed-
go/chapter6/goophr/concierge/common     [no test files]
```

The Concierge server

Let's try to post the book, *Hackers: Heroes of the Computer Revolution* to the Concierge endpoint, /api/feeder. We need to have the Concierge server running in another terminal window:

```
$ curl -X POST -d '{"title": "Hackers: Heroes of Computer Revolution",
"url": "http://www.gutenberg.org/cache/epub/729/pg729.txt"}'
http://localhost:8080/api/feeder | jq
     % Total    % Received % Xferd  Average Speed   Time    Time     Time
Current
                                    Dload  Upload   Total   Spent    Left
Speed
    100    162  100    51  100   111     51    111  0:00:01 --:--:--
0:00:01 54000
    {
      "code": 200,
      "msg": "Request is being processed."
    }
```

Next, let's see what happens on the server:

```
$ go run main.go
2017/11/18 21:05:57 INFO -  Adding API handlers...
2017/11/18 21:05:57 INFO -  Starting feeder...
2017/11/18 21:05:57 INFO -  Starting Goophr Concierge server on port
:8080...
// ...
adding to librarian: gutenberg-tm
adding to librarian: including
adding to librarian: make
adding to librarian: u.s
adding to librarian: project
adding to librarian: gutenberg
/...
```

Summary

In this chapter, we took an in-depth look at the `feeder` component of Concierge. We designed the system and used logical flow diagrams to understand how the various parts of the code interact. Next, we tested our code with tests and also with a real-world example.

In the next chapter, `Chapter 7`, *Goophr Librarian*, we will delve into the design and implementation of Goophr Librarian.

7
Goophr Librarian

In Chapter 6, *Goophr Concierge*, we built the endpoint responsible for accepting new documents and breaking them down into tokens to be used in the index. However, the current implementation of Concierge's `api.indexAdder` returns after printing the token to the console. In this chapter, we will implement Goophr Librarian, which can interact with the Concierge to accept tokens and also respond to token search queries.

In this chapter we will look at following topics:

- The standard indexing model
- The inverted indexing model
- The document indexer
- Query resolver APIs

The standard indexing model

Consider the index in a book. Each book will have its own index, which lists all the words in an alphabetical order showing their location within the book. However, if we want to keep track of word occurrences in multiple books, checking each book's index is quite inefficient. Let's look at an example.

An example – books with an index of words

Imagine we have three books: Book 1, Book 2, and Book 3, and the following are their respective indexes. The numbers beside each word represent which page the word occurs on:

```
* Book 1 (Index)
  - apple - 4, 10, 20
  - cat - 10, 21, 22
  - zebra - 15, 25, 63
* Book 2 (Index)
  - banana - 14, 19, 66
  - cake - 10, 37, 45
  - zebra - 67, 100, 129
* Book 3 (Index)
  - apple - 36, 55, 74
  - cake - 1, 9, 77
  - Whale - 11, 59, 79
```

Let's try to find three words from the books' indexes. A naïve approach might be to pick each book and scan it until we hit or miss the word:

- apple
- banana
- parrot

```
* Searching for 'apple'
  - Scanning Book 1. Result: Found.
  - Scanning Book 2. Result: Not Found.
  - Scanning Book 3. Result: Found.
* Searching for 'banana'
  - Scanning Book 1. Result: Not Found.
  - Scanning Book 2. Result: Found.
  - Scanning Book 3. Result: Not Found.
* Searching for 'parrot'
  - Scanning Book 1. Result: Not Found.
  - Scanning Book 2. Result: Not Found.
  - Scanning Book 3. Result: Not Found.
```

In a nutshell, for each of the terms, we iterated through every book index and searched for the word. We went through this whole process for every word including parrot, which is not present in any of the books! At first this might seem acceptable, performance-wise, but consider when we have over a million books to wade through; we realize that the approach would not be practical.

The inverted indexing model

Based on the preceding example, we can state the following:

- We need to have a quick lookup to determine if a word exists in our index
- For any given word, we need to have an efficient way to list all the books the word might be in

We can achieve these two niceties by using an inverted index. A standard index's mapping order is **book → word → occurrence (page, line, and so on)** as seen in the previous example. If we use an inverted index, the mapping order becomes **word → book → occurrence (page, line, and so on)**.

This change might not seem to be of great significance; however, it improves the look up a lot. Let's look at it with another example.

An example – the inverted index for words in books

Let's take the data from the same example as before but now classified according to an inverted index:

```
* apple
  - Book 1 - 4, 10, 20
  - Book 3 - 36, 55, 74
* banana
  - Book 2 - 14, 19, 66
* cake
  - Book 2 - 10, 37, 45
  - Book 3 - 1, 9, 77
* cat
  - Book 1 - 10, 21, 22
* whale
  - Book 3 - 11, 59, 79

* zebra
  - Book 1 - 15, 25, 63
  - Book 2 - 67, 100, 129
```

With this setup, we can efficiently answer following questions:

- Does a word exist in the index?
- What are all the books a word exists in?
- What pages does a word occur on in a given book?

Let's again try to find three words from the inverted index:

- `apple`
- `banana`
- `parrot`

```
* Searching for 'apple'
  - Scanning Inverted Index. Result: Found a list of books.
* Searching for 'banana'
  - Scanning Inverted Index. Result: Found a list of books.
* Searching for 'parrot'
  - Scanning Inverted Index. Result: Not Found.
```

To summarize, instead of going through each of the books, we do a single look up for each of the terms, determine if the term exists, and if it does, return the list of books which is our ultimate goal.

Ranking

Ranking and the relevance of search results is an interesting and complex topic. All major search engines have a dedicated group of software engineers and computer scientists who spend a lot of time and effort to ensure that their algorithms are most accurate.

For Goophr, we will simplify the ranking and limit it to the frequency of search terms. Higher the search term frequency, higher it ranks in the results.

Revisiting the API definition

Let's review Librarian's API definition:

```
openapi: 3.0.0
servers:
```

```
    - url: /api
info:
  title: Goophr Librarian API
  version: '1.0'
  description: |
    API responsible for indexing & communicating with Goophr Concierge.
paths:
  /index:
    post:
      description: |
        Add terms to index.
      responses:
        '200':
          description: |
            Terms were successfully added to the index.
        '400':
          description: >
            Request was not processed because payload was incomplete or
            incorrect.
          content:
            application/json:
              schema:
                $ref: '#/components/schemas/error'
      requestBody:
        content:
          application/json:
            schema:
              $ref: '#/components/schemas/terms'
        description: |
          List of terms to be added to the index.
        required: true
  /query:
    post:
      description: |
        Search for all terms in the payload.
      responses:
        '200':
          description: |
            Returns a list of all the terms along with their frequency,
            documents the terms appear in and link to the said documents.
          content:
            application/json:
              schema:
                $ref: '#/components/schemas/results'
        '400':
          description: >
            Request was not processed because payload was incomplete or
            incorrect.
```

```
            content:
              application/json:
                schema:
                  $ref: '#/components/schemas/error'
        parameters: []
  components:
    schemas:
      error:
        type: object
        properties:
          msg:
            type: string
      term:
        type: object
        required:
          - title
          - token
          - doc_id
          - line_index
          - token_index
        properties:
          title:
            description: |
              Title of the document to which the term belongs.
            type: string
          token:
            description: |
              The term to be added to the index.
            type: string
          doc_id:
            description: |
              The unique hash for each document.
            type: string
          line_index:
            description: |
              Line index at which the term occurs in the document.
            type: integer
          token_index:
            description: |
              Position of the term in the document.
            type: integer
      terms:
        type: object
        properties:
          code:
            type: integer
          data:
            type: array
```

```
      items:
         $ref: '#/components/schemas/term'
   results:
     type: object
     properties:
       count:
         type: integer
       data:
         type: array
         items:
           $ref: '#/components/schemas/result'
   result:
     type: object
     properties:
       doc_id:
         type: string
       score:
         type: integer
```

Based on the API definition, we can state the following:

- All communication is via the JSON format
- The two endpoints for Librarian are: /api/index and /api/query
- /api/index uses the POST method to add new tokens to the reverse index
- /api/query uses the POST method to receive search query terms and returns a list of all documents that the index contains

The document indexer – the REST API endpoint

The main aim of /api/index is to accept tokens from Concierge and add them to the index. So let's look at what we mean by "adding them to the index".

Document indexing can be defined as the following set of consecutive tasks:

1. We rely on the payload to provide us with all the meta information needed to store the token.
2. We follow down the inverted index tree, create any node in the path not yet created, and finally add the token details.

The query resolver – the REST API endpoint

The main aim of /api/query is to find the set of search terms in the inverted index and return a list of document IDs in decreasing order of relevance. Let's look at what we mean by "querying search terms" and "relevance".

Query resolution can be defined as the following set of consecutive tasks:

1. For each of the search terms, we would like to retrieve all available books in inverted index form.
2. Next, we would like to store the occurrence counts for all the words within each individual book in a simple look up table (map).
3. Once we have a map with books and their respective counts, we can convert the look up table into an array of ordered document IDs and their respective scores.

Code conventions

The code in this chapter is quite straightforward and it follows the same code conventions as in Chapter 6, *Goophr Concierge*. So let's jump right into the code.

Librarian source code

Now that we have discussed the design of Librarian in detail, let's look at the project structure and source code:

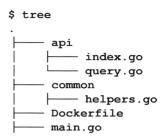

```
$ tree
.
├──── api
│     ├──── index.go
│     └──── query.go
├──── common
│     ├──── helpers.go
├──── Dockerfile
├──── main.go
```

Two directories and five files!

Now let's look at the source code for each of the files.

main.go

The source file is responsible for initializing routes, starting the index system and starting the web server:

```
package main

import (
    "net/http"

    "github.com/last-ent/distributed-go/chapter7/goophr/librarian/api"
    "github.com/last-ent/distributed-go/chapter7/goophr/librarian/common"
)

func main() {
    common.Log("Adding API handlers...")
    http.HandleFunc("/api/index", api.IndexHandler)
    http.HandleFunc("/api/query", api.QueryHandler)

    common.Log("Starting index...")
    api.StartIndexSystem()

    common.Log("Starting Goophr Librarian server on port :9090...")
    http.ListenAndServe(":9090", nil)
}
```

common/helpers.go

The source file consists of code that is speacialized to one handler.

```
package common

import (
    "fmt"
    "log"
)

func Log(msg string) {
    log.Println("INFO - ", msg)
}

func Warn(msg string) {
```

```
        log.Println("-------------------------")
        log.Println(fmt.Sprintf("WARN: %s", msg))
        log.Println("-------------------------")
}
```

api/index.go

Source file containing code to process and add new terms to the index.

```
package api

import (
    "bytes"
    "encoding/json"
    "fmt"
    "net/http"
)

// tPayload is used to parse the JSON payload consisting of Token data.
type tPayload struct {
    Token   string 'json:"token"'
    Title   string 'json:"title"'
    DocID   string 'json:"doc_id"'
    LIndex  int    'json:"line_index"'
    Index   int    'json:"token_index"'
}

type tIndex struct {
    Index   int
    LIndex  int
}

func (ti *tIndex) String() string {
    return fmt.Sprintf("i: %d, li: %d", ti.Index, ti.LIndex)
}

type tIndices []tIndex

// document - key in Indices represent Line Index.
type document struct {
    Count   int
    DocID   string
    Title   string
    Indices map[int]tIndices
}
```

```go
func (d *document) String() string {
    str := fmt.Sprintf("%s (%s): %d\n", d.Title, d.DocID, d.Count)
    var buffer bytes.Buffer

    for lin, tis := range d.Indices {
        var lBuffer bytes.Buffer
        for _, ti := range tis {
            lBuffer.WriteString(fmt.Sprintf("%s ", ti.String()))
        }
        buffer.WriteString(fmt.Sprintf("@%d -> %s\n", lin,
lBuffer.String()))
    }
    return str + buffer.String()
}


// documentCatalog - key represents DocID.
type documentCatalog map[string]*document

func (dc *documentCatalog) String() string {
    return fmt.Sprintf("%#v", dc)
}


// tCatalog - key in map represents Token.
type tCatalog map[string]documentCatalog

func (tc *tCatalog) String() string {
    return fmt.Sprintf("%#v", tc)
}


type tcCallback struct {
    Token string
    Ch    chan tcMsg
}


type tcMsg struct {
    Token string
    DC    documentCatalog
}


// pProcessCh is used to process /index's payload and start process to
add the token to catalog (tCatalog).
var pProcessCh chan tPayload

// tcGet is used to retrieve a token's catalog (documentCatalog).
var tcGet chan tcCallback

func StartIndexSystem() {
    pProcessCh = make(chan tPayload, 100)
```

```
        tcGet = make(chan tcCallback, 20)
        go tIndexer(pProcessCh, tcGet)
}

// tIndexer maintains a catalog of all tokens along with where they
// occur within documents.
func tIndexer(ch chan tPayload, callback chan tcCallback) {
    store := tCatalog{}
    for {
        select {
        case msg := <-callback:
            dc := store[msg.Token]
            msg.Ch <- tcMsg{
                DC:    dc,
                Token: msg.Token,
            }

        case pd := <-ch:
            dc, exists := store[pd.Token]
            if !exists {
                dc = documentCatalog{}
                store[pd.Token] = dc
            }

            doc, exists := dc[pd.DocID]
            if !exists {
                doc = &document{
                    DocID:   pd.DocID,
                    Title:   pd.Title,
                    Indices: map[int]tIndices{},
                }
                dc[pd.DocID] = doc
            }

            tin := tIndex{
                Index:  pd.Index,
                LIndex: pd.LIndex,
            }
            doc.Indices[tin.LIndex] = append(doc.Indices[tin.LIndex],
tin)
            doc.Count++
        }
    }
}

func IndexHandler(w http.ResponseWriter, r *http.Request) {
    if r.Method != "POST" {
        w.WriteHeader(http.StatusMethodNotAllowed)
```

```
        w.Write([]byte('{"code": 405, "msg": "Method Not Allowed."}'))
        return
    }

    decoder := json.NewDecoder(r.Body)
    defer r.Body.Close()

    var tp tPayload
    decoder.Decode(&tp)

    log.Printf("Token received%#v\n", tp)

    pProcessCh <- tp

    w.Write([]byte('{"code": 200, "msg": "Tokens are being added to
index."}'))
}
```

api/query.go

Source file contains code responsible for returning sorted results based on search terms.

```
package api

import (
    "encoding/json"
    "net/http"
    "sort"

    "github.com/last-ent/distributed-
go/chapter7/goophr/librarian/common"
)

type docResult struct {
    DocID   string    'json:"doc_id"'
    Score   int       'json:"doc_score"'
    Indices tIndices  'json:"token_indices"'
}

type result struct {
    Count int          'json:"count"'
    Data  []docResult  'json:"data"'
}

// getResults returns unsorted search results & a map of documents
containing tokens.
```

```
func getResults(out chan tcMsg, count int) tCatalog {
    tc := tCatalog{}
    for i := 0; i < count; i++ {
        dc := <-out
        tc[dc.Token] = dc.DC
    }
    close(out)

    return tc
}

func getFScores(docIDScore map[string]int) (map[int][]string, []int) {
    // fScore maps frequency score to set of documents.
    fScore := map[int][]string{}

    fSorted := []int{}

    for dID, score := range docIDScore {
        fs := fScore[score]
            fScore[score] = []string{}
        }
        fScore[score] = append(fs, dID)
        fSorted = append(fSorted, score)
    }

    sort.Sort(sort.Reverse(sort.IntSlice(fSorted)))

    return fScore, fSorted
}

func getDocMaps(tc tCatalog) (map[string]int, map[string]tIndices) {
    // docIDScore maps DocIDs to occurences of all tokens.
    // key: DocID.
    // val: Sum of all occurences of tokens so far.
    docIDScore := map[string]int{}
    docIndices := map[string]tIndices{}

    // for each token's catalog
    for _, dc := range tc {
        // for each document registered under the token
        for dID, doc := range dc {
            // add to docID score
            var tokIndices tIndices
            for _, tList := range doc.Indices {
                tokIndices = append(tokIndices, tList...)
            }
            docIDScore[dID] += doc.Count
```

```
            dti := docIndices[dID]
            docIndices[dID] = append(dti, tokIndices...)
        }
    }

    return docIDScore, docIndices
}

func sortResults(tc tCatalog) []docResult {
    docIDScore, docIndices := getDocMaps(tc)
    fScore, fSorted := getFScores(docIDScore)

    results := []docResult{}
    addedDocs := map[string]bool{}

    for _, score := range fSorted {
        for _, docID := range fScore[score] {
            if _, exists := addedDocs[docID]; exists {
                continue
            }
            results = append(results, docResult{
                DocID:    docID,
                Score:    score,
                Indices: docIndices[docID],
            })
            addedDocs[docID] = false
        }
    }
    return results
}

// getSearchResults returns a list of documents.
// They are listed in descending order of occurences.
func getSearchResults(sts []string) []docResult {

    callback := make(chan tcMsg)

    for _, st := range sts {
        go func(term string) {
            tcGet <- tcCallback{
                Token: term,
                Ch:    callback,
            }
        }(st)
    }

    cts := getResults(callback, len(sts))
    results := sortResults(cts)
```

```
        return results
}

func QueryHandler(w http.ResponseWriter, r *http.Request) {
    if r.Method != "POST" {
        w.WriteHeader(http.StatusMethodNotAllowed)
        w.Write([]byte('{"code": 405, "msg": "Method Not Allowed."}'))
        return
    }

    decoder := json.NewDecoder(r.Body)
    defer r.Body.Close()

    var searchTerms []string
    decoder.Decode(&searchTerms)

    results := getSearchResults(searchTerms)

    payload := result{
        Count: len(results),
        Data:  results,
    }

    if serializedPayload, err := json.Marshal(payload); err == nil {
        w.Header().Add("Content-Type", "application/json")
        w.Write(serializedPayload)
    } else {
        common.Warn("Unable to serialize all docs: " + err.Error())
        w.WriteHeader(http.StatusInternalServerError)
        w.Write([]byte('{"code": 500, "msg": "Error occurred while
trying to retrieve documents."}'))
    }
}
```

Testing Librarian

In order to test whether Librarian works as expected, we need to test two things:

1. Check if `/api/index` accepts index terms.
2. Check if `/api/query` returns the correct results and in the expected order.

We can test point 1 with the help of a separate program/script, `feeder.go`, and point 2 with simple cURL commands.

Testing feeder.go using /api/index

Here's the `feeder.go` script to check if `/api/index` accepts index terms:

```go
package main

import (
    "bytes"
    "encoding/json"
    "io/ioutil"
    "log"
    "net/http"
)

type tPayload struct {
    Token   string 'json:"token"'
    Title   string 'json:"title"'
    DocID   string 'json:"doc_id"'
    LIndex  int    'json:"line_index"'
    Index   int    'json:"token_index"'
}

type msgS struct {
    Code int    'json:"code"'
    Msg  string 'json:"msg"'
}

func main() {
    // Searching for "apple" should return Book 1 at the top of search
results.
    // Searching for "cake" should return Book 3 at the top.
    for bookX, terms := range map[string][]string{
        "Book 1": []string{"apple", "apple", "cat", "zebra"},
        "Book 2": []string{"banana", "cake", "zebra"},
```

```
            "Book 3": []string{"apple", "cake", "cake", "whale"},
    } {
        for lin, term := range terms {
            payload, _ := json.Marshal(tPayload{
                Token:  term,
                Title:  bookX + term,
                DocID:  bookX,
                LIndex: lin,
            })
            resp, err := http.Post(
                "http://localhost:9090/api/index",
                "application/json",
                bytes.NewBuffer(payload),
            )
            if err != nil {
                panic(err)
            }
            body, _ := ioutil.ReadAll(resp.Body)
            defer resp.Body.Close()

            var msg msgS
            json.Unmarshal(body, &msg)
            log.Println(msg)
        }
    }
}
```

The output from running `feeder.go` (with Librarian running in other window) is as follows:

```
$ go run feeder.go
2018/01/04 12:53:31 {200 Tokens are being added to index.}
2018/01/04 12:53:31 {200 Tokens are being added to index.}
2018/01/04 12:53:31 {200 Tokens are being added to index.}
2018/01/04 12:53:31 {200 Tokens are being added to index.}
2018/01/04 12:53:31 {200 Tokens are being added to index.}
2018/01/04 12:53:31 {200 Tokens are being added to index.}
2018/01/04 12:53:31 {200 Tokens are being added to index.}
2018/01/04 12:53:31 {200 Tokens are being added to index.}
2018/01/04 12:53:31 {200 Tokens are being added to index.}
2018/01/04 12:53:31 {200 Tokens are being added to index.}
2018/01/04 12:53:31 {200 Tokens are being added to index.}
```

The output from Librarian for the preceding program is as follows:

```
$ go run goophr/librarian/main.go
2018/01/04 12:53:25 INFO -  Adding API handlers...
2018/01/04 12:53:25 INFO -  Starting index...
2018/01/04 12:53:25 INFO -  Starting Goophr Librarian server on port
:9090...
2018/01/04 12:53:31 Token received api.tPayload{Token:"banana", Title:"Book
2banana", DocID:"Book 2", LIndex:0, Index:0}
2018/01/04 12:53:31 Token received api.tPayload{Token:"cake", Title:"Book
2cake", DocID:"Book 2", LIndex:1, Index:0}
2018/01/04 12:53:31 Token received api.tPayload{Token:"zebra", Title:"Book
2zebra", DocID:"Book 2", LIndex:2, Index:0}
2018/01/04 12:53:31 Token received api.tPayload{Token:"apple", Title:"Book
3apple", DocID:"Book 3", LIndex:0, Index:0}
2018/01/04 12:53:31 Token received api.tPayload{Token:"cake", Title:"Book
3cake", DocID:"Book 3", LIndex:1, Index:0}
2018/01/04 12:53:31 Token received api.tPayload{Token:"cake", Title:"Book
3cake", DocID:"Book 3", LIndex:2, Index:0}
2018/01/04 12:53:31 Token received api.tPayload{Token:"whale", Title:"Book
3whale", DocID:"Book 3", LIndex:3, Index:0}
2018/01/04 12:53:31 Token received api.tPayload{Token:"apple", Title:"Book
1apple", DocID:"Book 1", LIndex:0, Index:0}
2018/01/04 12:53:31 Token received api.tPayload{Token:"apple", Title:"Book
1apple", DocID:"Book 1", LIndex:1, Index:0}
2018/01/04 12:53:31 Token received api.tPayload{Token:"cat", Title:"Book
1cat", DocID:"Book 1", LIndex:2, Index:0}
2018/01/04 12:53:31 Token received api.tPayload{Token:"zebra", Title:"Book
1zebra", DocID:"Book 1", LIndex:3, Index:0}
```

Testing /api/query

In order to test /api/query we need to maintain the preceding state of the server to make useful queries:

```
$ # Querying for "apple"

$ curl -LX POST -d '["apple"]' localhost:9090/api/query | jq
  % Total    % Received % Xferd  Average Speed   Time    Time     Time
Current
                                 Dload  Upload   Total   Spent    Left
Speed
100   202  100   193  100     9    193      9  0:00:01 --:--:--  0:00:01
40400
{
  "count": 2,
```

```
      "data": [
        {
          "doc_id": "Book 1",
          "doc_score": 2,
          "token_indices": [
            {
              "Index": 0,
              "LIndex": 0
            },
            {
              "Index": 0,
              "LIndex": 1
            }
          ]
        },
        {
          "doc_id": "Book 3",
          "doc_score": 1,
          "token_indices": [
            {
              "Index": 0,
              "LIndex": 0
            }
          ]
        }
      ]
    }

$ # Querying for "cake"

$ curl -LX POST -d '["cake"]' localhost:9090/api/query | jq
  % Total    % Received % Xferd  Average Speed   Time    Time     Time
Current
                                 Dload  Upload   Total   Spent    Left
Speed
100   201  100   193  100     8    193        8  0:00:01 --:--:--  0:00:01
33500
{
  "count": 2,
  "data": [
    {
      "doc_id": "Book 3",
      "doc_score": 2,
      "token_indices": [
        {
          "Index": 0,
          "LIndex": 1
        },
```

```
        {
            "Index": 0,
            "LIndex": 2
        }
    ]
},
{
    "doc_id": "Book 2",
    "doc_score": 1,
    "token_indices": [
        {
            "Index": 0,
            "LIndex": 1
        }
    ]
}
]
}
```

Summary

In this chapter, we developed an understanding of inverted indices and implemented it for Librarian for the efficient storage and lookup of search terms. We also checked our implementation with the help of a script, feeder.go, and cURL commands.

In the next chapter, Chapter 8, *Deploying Goophr,* we will rewrite Concierge's api.indexAdder so that it can start sending the tokens to be indexed to Librarian. We will also revisit docker-compose.yaml so that we can have the complete application running and use/test it as a distributed system.

8

Deploying Goophr

In Chapter 6, *Goophr Concierge* and Chapter 7, *Goophr Librarian*, we built two components of Goophr: Concierge and Librarian. We took time to understand the rationale behind the design of each of the components and how they are expected to work together.

In this chapter, we will conclude building Goophr by achieving the following objectives:

- Update concierge/api/query.go so that Concierge can query multiple instances of Librarians for the search terms
- Update docker-compose.yaml so that we can run the complete Goophr system with little effort
- Test the setup by adding documents to the index and querying the index via the REST API

Updating Goophr Concierge

In order to make Concierge fully functional as per the design of Goophr, we need to do the following:

- Request search results from multiple Librarians
- Rank the combined search results

Let's discuss these points in detail.

Handle multiple Librarians

The core functionality of Goophr Librarian is to update the index and return relevant DocIDs based on the search terms. As we saw while implementing the codebase for Librarian, we need to update the index, retrieve relevant DocIDs, and then, based on relevance, sort them before returning query results. Many operations are involved and a lot of maps are being used for lookups and updates. These operations might seem trivial. However, as the size of the lookup table (map) increases, the performance of operations on the lookup table will start to decline. In order to avoid such a decline in performance, many approaches can be taken.

Our primary goal is to understand distributed systems in the context of Go, and, for this reason, we will split Librarian to handle only a certain set of the index. Partitioning is one of the standard techniques used in databases, where the database is split into multiple partitions. In our case, we we will have three instances of Librarian running, each of which is responsible for handling index for all tokens that are within character range, that are assigned to each of the partitions:

- a_m_librarian: Librarian responsible for tokens starting with character "A" to "M"
- n_z_librarian: Librarian responsible for tokens starting with character "N" to "Z"
- others_librarian: Librarian responsible for tokens starting with numbers

Aggregated search results

The next step would be to aggregate results of the search terms from the multiple instances of Librarian and return them as a payload to the query request. This would require us to do the following:

- Get a list of the URLs for all of the Librarians available
- Request search results from all the Librarians when a query is received
- Aggregate search results based on DocID
- Sort the results in descending order of relevance score
- Form and return the JSON payload as per the Swagger API definition

Now that we understand the rationale behind having multiple instances of Librarian, and how we are going to handle queries based on this new configuration, we can apply these changes to concierge/api/query.go.

Orchestrating with docker-compose

We have been running the servers for Librarian and Concierge on our system's localhost at hardcoded network port values. We haven't faced any issues with it so far. However, when we consider that we will be running three instances of Librarian, requiring to connect all of them to Concierge and be able to easily start and monitor the servers, we realize that there are a lot of moving parts. This can lead to unnecessary errors while operating the system. In order to make our life easy, we can rely on `docker-compose`, which will take care of all this complexity for us. All we have to do is define a configuration YAML file called `docker-compose.yaml` that will provide the following information:

- Identify the services we want to run together
- The location or name of the respective Dockerfile or Docker image for every service defined in the YAML file so that we can build Docker images for all of them and run them as containers
- Ports to expose for each of the running containers
- Any further environment variables we might want to inject into our server instances
- Ensure that Concierge's container has access to all other running containers

Environment variables and API ports

We mentioned that we will specify the port we want each of the containers to run on in `docker-compose.yaml`. However, we also need to update `{concierge, librarian}/main.go` so that they can start the servers at ports defined by environment variables. We will also need to update `concierge/query.go` so that it can access the Librarian instances on URLs and ports as defined by `docker-compose`.

The file server

In order to quickly test our setup by loading documents into the indexes, to be able to query the system and validate the query results, we will also be including a simple HTTP server that serves documents containing a few words.

The Goophr source code

In the previous two chapters, Chapter 6, *Goophr Concierge* and Chapter 7, *Goophr Librarian*, we discussed the code for Concierge and Librarian respectively. In order to run the complete Goophr application using docker-compose, we will need to merge the codebases of both Librarian and Concierge into a single codebase. The codebase will also include docker-compose.yaml and code for the file server.

In this chapter, we will not list the code for all the files in Librarian and Concierge but only the files with changes. Let's start by looking at the structure of the complete project:

```
$ tree -a
.
ε2;─── goophr
    ├─── concierge
    │   ├─── api
    │   │   ├─── feeder.go
    │   │   ├─── feeder_test.go
    │   │   └─── query.go
    │   ├─── common
    │   │   └─── helpers.go
    │   ├─── Dockerfile
    │   └─── main.go
    ├─── docker-compose.yaml
    ├─── .env
    ├─── librarian
    │   ├─── api
    │   │   ├─── index.go
    │   │   └─── query.go
    │   ├─── common
    │   │   └─── helpers.go
    │   ├─── Dockerfile
    │   └─── main.go
    └─── simple-server
        ├─── Dockerfile
        └─── main.go
8 directories, 15 files
```

librarian/main.go

We want to allow the Librarian to start on a custom port based on the environment variable, API_PORT, passed to it:

```
package main
```

```go
import (
    "fmt"
    "net/http"
    "os"

    "github.com/last-ent/distributed-go/chapter8/goophr/librarian/api"
    "github.com/last-ent/distributed-go/chapter8/goophr/librarian/common"
)

func main() {
    common.Log("Adding API handlers...")
    http.HandleFunc("/api/index", api.IndexHandler)
    http.HandleFunc("/api/query", api.QueryHandler)

    common.Log("Starting index...")
    api.StartIndexSystem()

    port := fmt.Sprintf(":%s", os.Getenv("API_PORT"))
    common.Log(fmt.Sprintf("Starting Goophr Librarian server on port
%s...", port))
    http.ListenAndServe(port, nil)
}
```

concierge/main.go

Allow Concierge to start on a custom port based on the environment variable, API_PORT, passed to it:

```go
package main

import (
    "fmt"
    "net/http"
    "os"

    "github.com/last-ent/distributed-go/chapter8/goophr/concierge/api"
    "github.com/last-ent/distributed-go/chapter8/goophr/concierge/common"
)

func main() {
    common.Log("Adding API handlers...")
    http.HandleFunc("/api/feeder", api.FeedHandler)
    http.HandleFunc("/api/query", api.QueryHandler)
```

```
    common.Log("Starting feeder...")
    api.StartFeederSystem()

    port := fmt.Sprintf(":%s", os.Getenv("API_PORT"))
    common.Log(fmt.Sprintf("Starting Goophr Concierge server on port
%s...", port))
    http.ListenAndServe(port, nil)
}
```

concierge/api/query.go

Query all the available Librarian instances to retrieve search query results, rank them in order, and then send back the results:

```
package api

import (
    "bytes"
    "encoding/json"
    "fmt"
    "io"
    "io/ioutil"
    "log"
    "net/http"
    "os"
    "sort"

    "github.com/last-ent/distributed-
go/chapter8/goophr/concierge/common"
)

var librarianEndpoints = map[string]string{}

func init() {
    librarianEndpoints["a-m"] = os.Getenv("LIB_A_M")
    librarianEndpoints["n-z"] = os.Getenv("LIB_N_Z")
    librarianEndpoints["*"] = os.Getenv("LIB_OTHERS")
}

type docs struct {
    DocID string 'json:"doc_id"'
    Score int    'json:"doc_score"'
}

type queryResult struct {
    Count int    'json:"count"'
```

```
        Data   []docs 'json:"data"'
}

func queryLibrarian(endpoint string, stBytes io.Reader, ch chan<-
queryResult) {
    resp, err := http.Post(
        endpoint+"/query",
        "application/json",
        stBytes,
    )
    if err != nil {
        common.Warn(fmt.Sprintf("%s -> %+v", endpoint, err))
        ch <- queryResult{}
        return
    }
    body, _ := ioutil.ReadAll(resp.Body)
    defer resp.Body.Close()

    var qr queryResult
    json.Unmarshal(body, &qr)
    log.Println(fmt.Sprintf("%s -> %#v", endpoint, qr))
    ch <- qr
}

func getResultsMap(ch <-chan queryResult) map[string]int {
    results := []docs{}
    for range librarianEndpoints {
        if result := <-ch; result.Count > 0 {
            results = append(results, result.Data...)
        }
    }

    resultsMap := map[string]int{}
    for _, doc := range results {
        docID := doc.DocID
        score := doc.Score
        if _, exists := resultsMap[docID]; !exists {
            resultsMap[docID] = 0
        }
        resultsMap[docID] = resultsMap[docID] + score
    }

    return resultsMap
}

func QueryHandler(w http.ResponseWriter, r *http.Request) {
    if r.Method != "POST" {
        w.WriteHeader(http.StatusMethodNotAllowed)
```

```
        w.Write([]byte('{"code": 405, "msg": "Method Not Allowed."}'))
        return
    }

    decoder := json.NewDecoder(r.Body)
    defer r.Body.Close()

    var searchTerms []string
    if err := decoder.Decode(&searchTerms); err != nil {
        common.Warn("Unable to parse request." + err.Error())

        w.WriteHeader(http.StatusBadRequest)
        w.Write([]byte('{"code": 400, "msg": "Unable to parse
payload."}'))
        return
    }

    st, err := json.Marshal(searchTerms)
    if err != nil {
        panic(err)
    }
    stBytes := bytes.NewBuffer(st)

    resultsCh := make(chan queryResult)

    for _, le := range librarianEndpoints {
        func(endpoint string) {
            go queryLibrarian(endpoint, stBytes, resultsCh)
        }(le)
    }

    resultsMap := getResultsMap(resultsCh)
    close(resultsCh)

    sortedResults := sortResults(resultsMap)

    payload, _ := json.Marshal(sortedResults)
    w.Header().Add("Content-Type", "application/json")
    w.Write(payload)

    fmt.Printf("%#v\n", sortedResults)
}

func sortResults(rm map[string]int) []document {
    scoreMap := map[int][]document{}
    ch := make(chan document)
    for docID, score := range rm {
        if _, exists := scoreMap[score]; !exists {
```

```
            scoreMap[score] = []document{}
        }

        dGetCh <- dMsg{
            DocID: docID,
            Ch:    ch,
        }
        doc := <-ch

        scoreMap[score] = append(scoreMap[score], doc)
    }

    close(ch)

    scores := []int{}
    for score := range scoreMap {
        scores = append(scores, score)
    }
    sort.Sort(sort.Reverse(sort.IntSlice(scores)))

    sortedResults := []document{}
    for _, score := range scores {
        resDocs := scoreMap[score]
        sortedResults = append(sortedResults, resDocs...)
    }
    return sortedResults
}
```

simple-server/Dockerfile

Let's use `Dockerfile` to create a simple file server:

```
FROM golang:1.10

ADD . /go/src/littlefs

WORKDIR /go/src/littlefs

RUN go install littlefs

ENTRYPOINT /go/bin/littlefs
```

simple-server/main.go

Let's look at a simple program that returns a set of words as an HTTP response based on `bookID`:

```go
package main

import (
    "log"
    "net/http"
)

func reqHandler(w http.ResponseWriter, r *http.Request) {
    books := map[string]string{
        "book1": 'apple apple cat zebra',
        "book2": 'banana cake zebra',
        "book3": 'apple cake cake whale',
    }

    bookID := r.URL.Path[1:]
    book, _ := books[bookID]
    w.Write([]byte(book))
}

func main() {

    log.Println("Starting File Server on Port :9876...")
    http.HandleFunc("/", reqHandler)
    http.ListenAndServe(":9876", nil)
}
```

docker-compose.yaml

This file will allow us to build, run, connect and stop our containers from a single interface.

```yaml
version: '3'

services:
  a_m_librarian:
    build: librarian/.
    environment:
      - API_PORT=${A_M_PORT}
    ports:
      - ${A_M_PORT}:${A_M_PORT}
  n_z_librarian:
```

```
    build: librarian/.
    environment:
      - API_PORT=${N_Z_PORT}
    ports:
      - ${N_Z_PORT}:${N_Z_PORT}
  others_librarian:
    build: librarian/.
    environment:
      - API_PORT=${OTHERS_PORT}
    ports:
      - ${OTHERS_PORT}:${OTHERS_PORT}
concierge:
  build: concierge/.
  environment:
    - API_PORT=${CONCIERGE_PORT}
    - LIB_A_M=http://a_m_librarian:${A_M_PORT}/api
    - LIB_N_Z=http://n_z_librarian:${N_Z_PORT}/api
    - LIB_OTHERS=http://others_librarian:${OTHERS_PORT}/api
  ports:
    - ${CONCIERGE_PORT}:${CONCIERGE_PORT}
  links:
    - a_m_librarian
    - n_z_librarian
    - others_librarian
    - file_server
file_server:
  build: simple-server/.
  ports:
    - ${SERVER_PORT}:${SERVER_PORT}
```

Linked services can be referred to using the service name as the domain name.

.env

`.env` is used within `docker-compose.yaml` to load template variables. It follows the format of `<template-variable>=<value>`:

```
CONCIERGE_PORT=9090
A_M_PORT=6060
N_Z_PORT=7070
OTHERS_PORT=8080
SERVER_PORT=9876
```

We can view the `docker-compose.yaml` with substituted values by running the following command:

```
$ pwd
GO-WORKSPACE/src/github.com/last-ent/distributed-go/chapter8/goophr
$ docker-compose config
services:
  a_m_librarian:
    build:
      context: /home/entux/Documents/Code/GO-WORKSPACE/src/github.com/last-
ent/distributed-go/chapter8/goophr/librarian
    environment:
      API_PORT: '6060'
    ports:
    - 6060:6060/tcp
  concierge:
    build:
      context: /home/entux/Documents/Code/GO-WORKSPACE/src/github.com/last-
ent/distributed-go/chapter8/goophr/concierge
    environment:
      API_PORT: '9090'
      LIB_A_M: http://a_m_librarian:6060/api
      LIB_N_Z: http://n_z_librarian:7070/api
      LIB_OTHERS: http://others_librarian:8080/api
    links:
    - a_m_librarian
    - n_z_librarian
    - others_librarian
    - file_server
    ports:
    - 9090:9090/tcp
  file_server:
    build:
      context: /home/entux/Documents/Code/GO-WORKSPACE/src/github.com/last-
ent/distributed-go/chapter8/goophr/simple-server
    ports:
    - 9876:9876/tcp
  n_z_librarian:
    build:
      context: /home/entux/Documents/Code/GO-WORKSPACE/src/github.com/last-
ent/distributed-go/chapter8/goophr/librarian
    environment:
      API_PORT: '7070'
    ports:
    - 7070:7070/tcp
  others_librarian:
    build:
```

```
        context: /home/entux/Documents/Code/GO-WORKSPACE/src/github.com/last-
    ent/distributed-go/chapter8/goophr/librarian
        environment:
            API_PORT: '8080'
        ports:
        - 8080:8080/tcp
    version: '3.0'
```

Running Goophr with docker-compose

Now that we have everything in place, let's start the complete application:

```
$ docker-compose up --build
Building a_m_librarian
...
Successfully built 31e0b1a7d3fc
Building n_z_librarian
...
Successfully built 31e0b1a7d3fc
Building others_librarian
...
Successfully built 31e0cdb1a7d3fc
Building file_server
...
Successfully built 244831d4b86a
Building concierge
...
Successfully built ba1167718d29
Starting goophr_a_m_librarian_1 ...
Starting goophr_file_server_1 ...
Starting goophr_a_m_librarian_1
Starting goophr_n_z_librarian_1 ...
Starting goophr_others_librarian_1 ...
Starting goophr_file_server_1
Starting goophr_n_z_librarian_1
Starting goophr_others_librarian_1 ... done
Starting goophr_concierge_1 ...
Starting goophr_concierge_1 ... done
Attaching to goophr_a_m_librarian_1, goophr_n_z_librarian_1,
goophr_file_server_1, goophr_others_librarian_1, goophr_concierge_1
a_m_librarian_1    | 2018/01/21 19:21:00 INFO -  Adding API handlers...
a_m_librarian_1    | 2018/01/21 19:21:00 INFO -  Starting index...
a_m_librarian_1    | 2018/01/21 19:21:00 INFO -  Starting Goophr Librarian
server on port :6060...
n_z_librarian_1    | 2018/01/21 19:21:00 INFO -  Adding API handlers...
others_librarian_1 | 2018/01/21 19:21:01 INFO -  Adding API handlers...
```

```
others_librarian_1  | 2018/01/21 19:21:01 INFO -  Starting index...
others_librarian_1  | 2018/01/21 19:21:01 INFO -  Starting Goophr Librarian
server on port :8080...
n_z_librarian_1     | 2018/01/21 19:21:00 INFO -  Starting index...
n_z_librarian_1     | 2018/01/21 19:21:00 INFO -  Starting Goophr Librarian
server on port :7070...
file_server_1       | 2018/01/21 19:21:01 Starting File Server on Port
:9876...
concierge_1         | 2018/01/21 19:21:02 INFO -  Adding API handlers...
concierge_1         | 2018/01/21 19:21:02 INFO -  Starting feeder...
concierge_1         | 2018/01/21 19:21:02 INFO -  Starting Goophr Concierge
server on port :9090...
```

Adding documents to Goophr

Since we have three documents in our file server, we can add them to Goophr using the
following `curl` commands:

```
$ curl -LX POST -d '{"url":"http://file_server:9876/book1","title":"Book
1"}' localhost:9090/api/feeder | jq  &&
> curl -LX POST -d '{"url":"http://file_server:9876/book2","title":"Book
2"}' localhost:9090/api/feeder | jq  &&
> curl -LX POST -d '{"url":"http://file_server:9876/book3","title":"Book
3"}' localhost:9090/api/feeder | jq
  % Total    % Received % Xferd  Average Speed   Time    Time     Time
Current
                                 Dload  Upload   Total   Spent    Left
Speed
100   107  100    51  100    56     51     56  0:00:01 --:--:--  0:00:01
104k
{
  "code": 200,
  "msg": "Request is being processed."
}
  % Total    % Received % Xferd  Average Speed   Time    Time     Time
Current
                                 Dload  Upload   Total   Spent    Left
Speed
100   107  100    51  100    56     51     56  0:00:01 --:--:--  0:00:01
21400
{
  "code": 200,
  "msg": "Request is being processed."
}
  % Total    % Received % Xferd  Average Speed   Time    Time     Time
Current
```

```
                                  Dload   Upload   Total   Spent   Left
Speed
100    107   100     51  100      56      51       56   0:00:01 --:--:--  0:00:01
21400
{
  "code": 200,
  "msg": "Request is being processed."
}
```

The following are the logs for the preceding cURL requests as seen by docker-compose:

```
n_z_librarian_1         | 2018/01/21 19:29:23 Token received
api.tPayload{Token:"zebra", Title:"Book 1",
DocID:"6911b2295fd23c77fca7d739c00735b14cf80d3c", LIndex:0, Index:3}
concierge_1             | adding to librarian: zebra
concierge_1             | adding to librarian: apple
concierge_1             | adding to librarian: apple
concierge_1             | adding to librarian: cat
concierge_1             | 2018/01/21 19:29:23 INFO - Request was posted to
Librairan. Msg:{"code": 200, "msg": "Tokens are being added to index."}
...
concierge_1             | 2018/01/21 19:29:23 INFO - Request was posted to
Librairan. Msg:{"code": 200, "msg": "Tokens are being added to index."}
a_m_librarian_1         | 2018/01/21 19:29:23 Token received
api.tPayload{Token:"apple", Title:"Book 1",
DocID:"6911b2295fd23c77fca7d739c00735b14cf80d3c", LIndex:0, Index:0}
...
n_z_librarian_1         | 2018/01/21 19:29:23 Token received
api.tPayload{Token:"zebra", Title:"Book 2",
DocID:"fbf2b6c400680389459dff13283cb01dfe9be7d6", LIndex:0, Index:2}
concierge_1             | adding to librarian: zebra
concierge_1             | adding to librarian: banana
concierge_1             | adding to librarian: cake
...
concierge_1             | adding to librarian: whale
concierge_1             | adding to librarian: apple
concierge_1             | adding to librarian: cake
concierge_1             | adding to librarian: cake
...
concierge_1             | 2018/01/21 19:29:23 INFO - Request was posted to
Librairan. Msg:{"code": 200, "msg": "Tokens are being added to index."}
```

Searching for keywords with Goophr

Now that we have the complete application running and some documents in the index, let's test it by searching for some of the keywords. The following is the list of terms we will be searching for and the expected order:

- **"apple"** - book1 (score: 2), book 3 (score: 1)
- **"cake"** - book 3 (score: 2), book 2 (score: 1)
- **"apple"**, **"cake"** - book 3 (score 3), book 1 (score: 2), book 2 (score: 1)

Search – "apple"

Let us search for "`apple`" alone using the cURL command:

```
$ curl -LX POST -d '["apple"]' localhost:9090/api/query | jq
  % Total    % Received % Xferd  Average Speed   Time    Time     Time
Current
                                 Dload  Upload   Total   Spent    Left
Speed
100   124  100   115  100     9    115       9  0:00:01 --:--:--  0:00:01
41333
[
  {
    "title": "Book 1",
    "url": "http://file_server:9876/book1"
  },
  {
    "title": "Book 3",
    "url": "http://file_server:9876/book3"
  }
]
```

The following are the `docker-compose` logs when we search for "`apple`":

```
concierge_1          | 2018/01/21 20:27:11 http://n_z_librarian:7070/api ->
api.queryResult{Count:0, Data:[]api.docs{}}
concierge_1          | 2018/01/21 20:27:11 http://a_m_librarian:6060/api ->
api.queryResult{Count:2,
Data:[]api.docs{api.docs{DocID:"7bded23abfac73630d247b6ad24370214fe1811c",
Score:2}, api.docs{DocID:"3c9c56d31ccd51bc7ac0011020819ef38ccd74a4",
Score:1}}}
concierge_1          | []api.document{api.document{Doc:"apple apple cat
zebra", Title:"Book 1", DocID:"7bded23abfac73630d247b6ad24370214fe1811c",
URL:"http://file_server:9876/book1"}, api.document{Doc:"apple cake cake
```

```
whale", Title:"Book 3", DocID:"3c9c56d31ccd51bc7ac0011020819ef38ccd74a4",
URL:"http://file_server:9876/book3"}}
concierge_1          | 2018/01/21 20:27:11 http://others_librarian:8080/api
-> api.queryResult{Count:0, Data:[]api.docs{}}
```

Search – "cake"

Let us search for "cake" alone using the cURL command:

```
$ curl -LX POST -d '["cake"]' localhost:9090/api/query | jq
  % Total    % Received % Xferd  Average Speed   Time    Time     Time
Current
                                 Dload  Upload   Total   Spent    Left
Speed
100   123  100   115  100     8    115       8  0:00:01 --:--:--  0:00:01
61500
[
  {
    "title": "Book 3",
    "url": "http://file_server:9876/book3"
  },
  {
    "title": "Book 2",
    "url": "http://file_server:9876/book2"
  }
]
```

The following are the `docker-compose` logs when we search for "cake":

```
concierge_1          | 2018/01/21 20:30:13 http://a_m_librarian:6060/api ->
api.queryResult{Count:2,
Data:[]api.docs{api.docs{DocID:"3c9c56d31ccd51bc7ac0011020819ef38ccd74a4",
Score:2}, api.docs{DocID:"28582e23c02ed3f14f8b4bdae97f91106273c0fc",
Score:1}}}
concierge_1          | 2018/01/21 20:30:13 --------------------------
concierge_1          | 2018/01/21 20:30:13 WARN:
http://others_librarian:8080/api -> Post
http://others_librarian:8080/api/query: http: ContentLength=8 with Body
length 0
concierge_1          | 2018/01/21 20:30:13 --------------------------
concierge_1          | 2018/01/21 20:30:13 http://n_z_librarian:7070/api ->
api.queryResult{Count:0, Data:[]api.docs{}}
concierge_1          | []api.document{api.document{Doc:"apple cake cake
whale", Title:"Book 3", DocID:"3c9c56d31ccd51bc7ac0011020819ef38ccd74a4",
URL:"http://file_server:9876/book3"}, api.document{Doc:"banana cake zebra",
Title:"Book 2", DocID:"28582e23c02ed3f14f8b4bdae97f91106273c0fc",
```

```
URL:"http://file_server:9876/book2"}}
```

Search – "apple", "cake"

Let us search for "apple" and "cake" together using the cURL command:

```
$ curl -LX POST -d '["cake", "apple"]' localhost:9090/api/query | jq
  % Total    % Received % Xferd  Average Speed   Time    Time     Time
Current
                                 Dload  Upload   Total   Spent    Left
Speed
100   189  100   172  100    17    172     17  0:00:01 --:--:--  0:00:01
27000
[
  {
    "title": "Book 3",
    "url": "http://file_server:9876/book3"
  },
  {
    "title": "Book 1",
    "url": "http://file_server:9876/book1"
  },
  {
    "title": "Book 2",
    "url": "http://file_server:9876/book2"
  }
]
```

The following are the docker-compose logs when we search for "apple" and "cake":

```
concierge_1          | 2018/01/21 20:31:06 http://a_m_librarian:6060/api ->
api.queryResult{Count:3,
Data:[]api.docs{api.docs{DocID:"3c9c56d31ccd51bc7ac0011020819ef38ccd74a4",
Score:3}, api.docs{DocID:"7bded23abfac73630d247b6ad24370214fe1811c",
Score:2}, api.docs{DocID:"28582e23c02ed3f14f8b4bdae97f91106273c0fc",
Score:1}}}
concierge_1          | 2018/01/21 20:31:06 http://n_z_librarian:7070/api ->
api.queryResult{Count:0, Data:[]api.docs{}}
concierge_1          | 2018/01/21 20:31:06 --------------------------
concierge_1          | 2018/01/21 20:31:06 WARN:
http://others_librarian:8080/api -> Post
http://others_librarian:8080/api/query: http: ContentLength=16 with Body
length 0
concierge_1          | 2018/01/21 20:31:06 --------------------------
concierge_1          | []api.document{api.document{Doc:"apple cake cake
whale", Title:"Book 3", DocID:"3c9c56d31ccd51bc7ac0011020819ef38ccd74a4",
```

```
URL:"http://file_server:9876/book3"}, api.document{Doc:"apple apple cat
zebra", Title:"Book 1", DocID:"7bded23abfac73630d247b6ad24370214fe1811c",
URL:"http://file_server:9876/book1"}, api.document{Doc:"banana cake zebra",
Title:"Book 2", DocID:"28582e23c02ed3f14f8b4bdae97f91106273c0fc",
URL:"http://file_server:9876/book2"}}
```

Individual logs with docker-compose

We can also view logs of each service separately. The following are the logs for Concierge:

```
$ docker-compose logs concierge
Attaching to goophr_concierge_1
concierge_1          | 2018/01/21 19:18:30 INFO -  Adding API handlers...
concierge_1          | 2018/01/21 19:18:30 INFO -  Starting feeder...
concierge_1          | 2018/01/21 19:18:30 INFO -  Starting Goophr Concierge
server on port :9090...
concierge_1          | 2018/01/21 19:21:02 INFO -  Adding API handlers...
concierge_1          | 2018/01/21 19:21:02 INFO -  Starting feeder...
concierge_1          | 2018/01/21 19:21:02 INFO -  Starting Goophr Concierge
server on port :9090...
concierge_1          | adding to librarian: zebra
concierge_1          | adding to librarian: apple
concierge_1          | adding to librarian: apple
concierge_1          | adding to librarian: cat
concierge_1          | 2018/01/21 19:25:40 INFO -  Request was posted to
Librairan. Msg:{"code": 200, "msg": "Tokens are being added to index."}
concierge_1          | 2018/01/21 20:31:06 http://a_m_librarian:6060/api ->
api.queryResult{Count:3,
Data:[]api.docs{api.docs{DocID:"3c9c56d31ccd51bc7ac0011020819ef38ccd74a4",
Score:3}, api.docs{DocID:"7bded23abfac73630d247b6ad24370214fe1811c",
Score:2}, api.docs{DocID:"28582e23c02ed3f14f8b4bdae97f91106273c0fc",
Score:1}}}
concierge_1          | 2018/01/21 20:31:06 http://n_z_librarian:7070/api ->
api.queryResult{Count:0, Data:[]api.docs{}}
concierge_1          | 2018/01/21 20:31:06 --------------------------
concierge_1          | 2018/01/21 20:31:06 WARN:
http://others_librarian:8080/api -> Post
http://others_librarian:8080/api/query: http: ContentLength=16 with Body
length 0
concierge_1          | 2018/01/21 20:31:06 --------------------------
concierge_1          | []api.document{api.document{Doc:"apple cake cake
whale", Title:"Book 3", DocID:"3c9c56d31ccd51bc7ac0011020819ef38ccd74a4",
URL:"http://file_server:9876/book3"}, api.document{Doc:"apple apple cat
zebra", Title:"Book 1", DocID:"7bded23abfac73630d247b6ad24370214fe1811c",
URL:"http://file_server:9876/book1"}, api.document{Doc:"banana cake zebra",
Title:"Book 2", DocID:"28582e23c02ed3f14f8b4bdae97f91106273c0fc",
```

```
URL:"http://file_server:9876/book2"}}
```

Authorization on a web server

Our search application trusts every incoming request. However, sometimes restricting access might be the right way to go. It would be desirable if, for every incoming request, we could accept and identify requests from certain users. This can be achieved using **authorization tokens (auth tokens)**. An auth token is a secret code/phrase sent in the header for the key, **Authorization**.

Authorization and auth tokens are deep and important topics. It would not be possible to cover the complexity of the subject in this section. Instead, we will build a simple server that will make use of auth tokens to accept or reject a request. Let us look at the source code.

secure/secure.go

`secure.go` shows the logic for the simple server. It has been divided into four functions:

- The `requestHandler` function to respond to incoming HTTP requests.
- The `isAuthorized` function to check if the incoming request is authorized.
- The `getAuthorizedUser` function to check if the token has an associated user. If the token does not have an associated user, then the token is considered to be invalid.
- The `main` function to start the server.

Now let's look at the code:

```
// secure/secure.go
package main

import (
    "fmt"
    "log"
    "net/http"
    "strings"
)

var authTokens = map[string]string{
    "AUTH-TOKEN-1": "User 1",
    "AUTH-TOKEN-2": "User 2",
}
```

```go
// getAuthorizedUser tries to retrieve user for the given token.
func getAuthorizedUser(token string) (string, error) {
    var err error

    user, valid := authTokens[token]
    if !valid {
        err = fmt.Errorf("Auth token '%s' does not exist.", token)
    }

    return user, err
}

// isAuthorized checks request to ensure that it has Authorization header
// with defined value: "Bearer AUTH-TOKEN"
func isAuthorized(r *http.Request) bool {
    rawToken := r.Header["Authorization"]
    if len(rawToken) != 1 {
        return false
    }

    authToken := strings.Split(rawToken[0], " ")
    if !(len(authToken) == 2 && authToken[0] == "Bearer") {
        return false
    }

    user, err := getAuthorizedUser(authToken[1])
    if err != nil {
        log.Printf("Error: %s", err)
        return false
    }

    log.Printf("Successful request made by '%s'", user)
    return true
}

var success = []byte("Received authorized request.")
var failure = []byte("Received unauthorized request.")

func requestHandler(w http.ResponseWriter, r *http.Request) {
    if isAuthorized(r) {
        w.Write(success)
    } else {
        w.WriteHeader(http.StatusUnauthorized)
        w.Write(failure)
    }
}

func main() {
```

```
    http.HandleFunc("/", requestHandler)
    fmt.Println("Starting server @ http://localhost:8080")
    http.ListenAndServe(":8080", nil)
}
```

secure/secure_test.go

Next, we will try to test the logic we have written in secure.go using unit tests. A good practice is to test each of the functions for all possible cases of success and failure. The test names explain the intent of the test, so let's look at the code:

```
// secure/secure_test.go

package main

import (
    "net/http"
    "net/http/httptest"
    "testing"
)

func TestIsAuthorizedSuccess(t *testing.T) {
    req, err := http.NewRequest("GET", "http://example.com", nil)
    if err != nil {
        t.Error("Unable to create request")
    }

    req.Header["Authorization"] = []string{"Bearer AUTH-TOKEN-1"}

    if isAuthorized(req) {
        t.Log("Request with correct Auth token was correctly processed.")
    } else {
        t.Error("Request with correct Auth token failed.")
    }
}

func TestIsAuthorizedFailTokenType(t *testing.T) {
    req, err := http.NewRequest("GET", "http://example.com", nil)
    if err != nil {
        t.Error("Unable to create request")
    }

    req.Header["Authorization"] = []string{"Token AUTH-TOKEN-1"}

    if isAuthorized(req) {
        t.Error("Request with incorrect Auth token type was successfully
```

```
processed.")
    } else {
        t.Log("Request with incorrect Auth token type failed as expected.")
    }
}

func TestIsAuthorizedFailToken(t *testing.T) {
    req, err := http.NewRequest("GET", "http://example.com", nil)
    if err != nil {
        t.Error("Unable to create request")
    }

    req.Header["Authorization"] = []string{"Token WRONG-AUTH-TOKEN"}

    if isAuthorized(req) {
        t.Error("Request with incorrect Auth token was successfully
processed.")
    } else {
        t.Log("Request with incorrect Auth token failed as expected.")
    }
}

func TestRequestHandlerFailToken(t *testing.T) {
    req, err := http.NewRequest("GET", "http://example.com", nil)
    if err != nil {
        t.Error("Unable to create request")
    }

    req.Header["Authorization"] = []string{"Token WRONG-AUTH-TOKEN"}

    // http.ResponseWriter it is an interface hence we use
    // httptest.NewRecorder which implements the interface
http.ResponseWriter
    rr := httptest.NewRecorder()
    requestHandler(rr, req)

    if rr.Code == 401 {
        t.Log("Request with incorrect Auth token failed as expected.")
    } else {
        t.Error("Request with incorrect Auth token was successfully
processed.")
    }
}

func TestGetAuthorizedUser(t *testing.T) {
    if user, err := getAuthorizedUser("AUTH-TOKEN-2"); err != nil {
        t.Errorf("Couldn't find User 2. Error: %s", err)
    } else if user != "User 2" {
```

```
            t.Errorf("Found incorrect user: %s", user)
        } else {
            t.Log("Found User 2.")
        }
    }

    func TestGetAuthorizedUserFail(t *testing.T) {
        if user, err := getAuthorizedUser("WRONG-AUTH-TOKEN"); err == nil {
            t.Errorf("Found user for invalid token!. User: %s", user)
        } else if err.Error() != "Auth token 'WRONG-AUTH-TOKEN' does not
    exist." {
            t.Errorf("Error message does not match.")
        } else {
            t.Log("Got expected error message for invalid auth token")
        }
    }
```

Test results

Finally, let us run the tests and see if they produce the expected results:

```
$ go test -v ./...
=== RUN   TestIsAuthorizedSuccess
2018/02/19 00:08:06 Successful request made by 'User 1'
--- PASS: TestIsAuthorizedSuccess (0.00s)
        secure_test.go:18: Request with correct Auth token was correctly
processed.
=== RUN   TestIsAuthorizedFailTokenType
--- PASS: TestIsAuthorizedFailTokenType (0.00s)
        secure_test.go:35: Request with incorrect Auth token type failed as
expected.
=== RUN   TestIsAuthorizedFailToken
--- PASS: TestIsAuthorizedFailToken (0.00s)
        secure_test.go:50: Request with incorrect Auth token failed as
expected.
=== RUN   TestRequestHandlerFailToken
--- PASS: TestRequestHandlerFailToken (0.00s)
        secure_test.go:68: Request with incorrect Auth token failed as
expected.
=== RUN   TestGetAuthorizedUser
--- PASS: TestGetAuthorizedUser (0.00s)
        secure_test.go:80: Found User 2.
=== RUN   TestGetAuthorizedUserFail
--- PASS: TestGetAuthorizedUserFail (0.00s)
        secure_test.go:90: Got expected error message for invalid auth
token
```

```
PASS
ok      chapter8/secure      0.003s
```

Summary

In this chapter, we started by trying to understand why we need to run multiple instances of Goophr Librarian. Next, we looked at how to implement the updated `concierge/api/query.go` so that it can work with multiple instances of Librarian. Then we looked into why using `docker-compose` to orchestrate the application might be a good idea and what may be the various factors to keep in mind to make it work. We also updated the Librarian and Concierge codebase so that they would work seamlessly with `docker-compose`. Finally, we tested the complete application using a few small documents and reasoning about the expected order of results.

We were able to orchestrate all the servers we needed to run the complete Goophr application on our local machine using `docker-compose`. However, designing the architecture of a resilient web application to withstand heavy user traffic on the internet can be quite challenging. `Chapter 9`, *Foundations of Web Scale Architecture* tries to address this issue by providing some basic knowledge of things to take into consideration while designing for the web.

9
Foundations of Web Scale Architecture

Chapter 5, *Introducing Goophr*, Chapter 6, *Goophr Concierge*, and Chapter 7, *Goophr Librarian* were about the design and implementation of a distributed search index system, starting from basic concepts to running individual components and verifying that they work as expected. In Chapter 8, *Deploying Goophr*, we connected the various components with the help of **docker-compose** so that we could launch and connect all the components in an easy and reliable manner. We have achieved quite a lot in the past four chapters, but you may have noticed that we ran everything on a single machine, most likely our laptop or desktop.

Ideally, we should next try to prepare our distributed system to work reliably under a heavy user load and expose it over the web for general use. However, the reality is that we will have to make a lot of upgrades to our current system to make it reliable and resilient enough to be able to work under real-world traffic.

In this chapter, we are going to look at various factors we should keep in mind while we try to design for the web. We will be looking at:

- Scaling a web application
- Monolith app versus microservices
- Deployment options

Scaling a web application

In this chapter, we will not be discussing Goophr but instead a simple web application for blogging so that we can concentrate on scaling it for the web. Such an application may consist of a single server instance running the database and the blog server.

Scaling a web application is an intricate topic, and we will devote a lot of time to this very subject. As we shall see throughout this section, there are multiple ways to scale a system:

- Scaling the system as a whole
- Splitting up the system and scaling individual components
- Choosing specific solutions to better scale the system

Let's start with the most basic setup, a single server instance.

The single server instance

A single server setup will generally consist of:

- A web server to serve web pages and handle server-side logic
- A database to save all user data (blog posts, user login details, and so on) related to the blog

The following figure shows what such a server would look like:

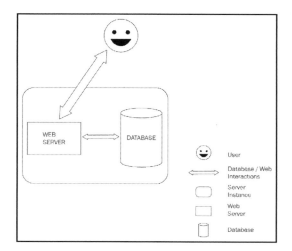

The figure shows a simple setup where the user interacts with the blog server, which will be interacting with a database internally. This setup of a database and blog server on the same instance will be efficient and responsive only up to a certain number of users.

As the system starts to slow down or storage starts to fill up, we can redeploy our application (database and blog server) on to a different server instance with more storage, RAM, and CPU power; this is known as **vertical scaling**. As you may suspect, this can be time consuming and an inconvenient way of upgrading your server. Wouldn't it be better if we could stave off this upgrade for as long as possible?

An important point to think about is that the issue might be due to any combination of the following factors:

- Out of memory due to the database or blog server
- Performance degradation due to the web server or database requiring more CPU cycles
- Out of storage space due to the database

Scaling the complete application for any of the preceding factors isn't an optimal way to deal with the issue because we are spending a lot of money where we could have solved the issue with far fewer resources! So how should we fashion our system so that we can solve the right problem in the right manner?

Separate layers for the web and database

If we take the three issues stated earlier, we can solve each of them in one or two ways. Let's look at them first:

Issue #1: Out of memory

Solution:

- **Due to the database**: Increase RAM for the database
- **Due to the blog server**: Increase RAM for the blog server

Issue #2: Performance degradation

Solution:

- **Due to the database**: Increase the CPU power for the database
- **Due to the blog server**: Increase the CPU power for the blog server

Issue #3: Out of storage space

Solution:

- **Due to the database**: Increase the storage space for the database

Using this listing, we can upgrade our system as and when required for a particular problem we are facing. However, we first need to correctly identify the component that is causing the issue. For this reason, even before we start scaling our application vertically, we should separate our database from our web server as shown in this figure:

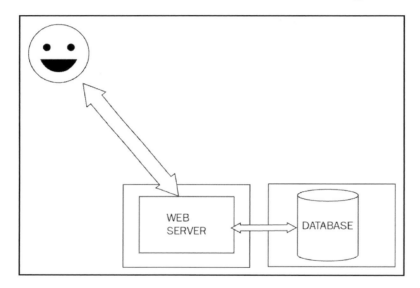

This new setup with the database and the blog server on separate server instances would enable us to monitor which component is having an issue and vertically scale only that particular component. We should be able to serve a larger user traffic with this new setup.

However, as the load on the server increases, we might have other issues on our hands. For example, what would happen if our blog server were to become unresponsive? We would no longer be able to serve blog posts and no one would be able to post comments on said blog posts. This is a situation no one wants to face. Wouldn't it be nice if we could keep serving traffic even if the blog server were down?

Multiple server instances

Serving a large traffic of users with a single server instance for our blog server or any application (business logic) server is dangerous because we are essentially creating a single point of failure. The most logical and simplest way to avoid such a situation is to have duplicate instances of our blog server to handle incoming user traffic. This approach of scaling a single server to multiple instances is known as **horizontal scaling**. However, this raises the question: how can we reliably distribute the traffic between the various instances of our blog server? For this we use a **load balancer**.

The load balancer

A load balancer is a type of HTTP server responsible for distributing traffic (routing) to various web servers based on the rules defined by the developer. A load balancer, in general, is a very fast and specialized application. Trying to implement similar logic in a web server might not be optimal because the resources available to your web server have to be split between handling requests for your business logic and requests that need to be routed. Also, a load balancer provides us with a lot of features out of the box such as these:

- **Load balancing algorithms**: The following are some algorithms for load balancing:
    - **Random**: Distribute randomly across the servers.
    - **Round robin**: Distribute equally and sequentially across servers.
    - **Asymmetric load**: Distribute between servers in certain proportions. For example, for 100 requests, send 80 to Server A and 20 to Server B.
    - **Least connections**: Send a new request to the server with the least number of active connections (an asymmetric load can also be integrated with least connections).
- **Session persistence**: Imagine an e-commerce site where a user has added items to his shopping cart and the information about items in the cart is stored on, Server A. However, when the user wants to complete the purchase, the request is sent to a different server, Server B! This would be an issue for the user because all details related to his shopping cart is on Server A. Load balancers have the provision to ensure that such requests are redirected to the relevant server.

- **HTTP compression**: Load balancers also have the provision to compress the outgoing response using `gzip` so that it has less data to send to the user. This tends to greatly improve the user experience.
- **HTTP caching**: For sites that serve more than REST API content, a lot of files can be cached because they do not change as often and cached content can be delivered much faster.

Depending on which load balancer is being used, they can provide a lot more features than the ones stated above. This should give an idea about the capability of a load balancer.

The following figure shows how a load balancer and multiple servers might work together:

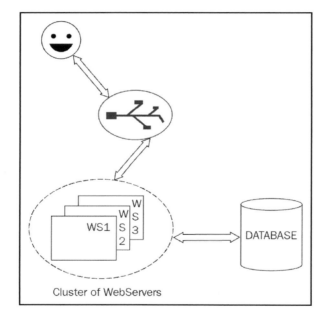

Cluster of WebServers

The user's requests reach the load balancer, which then routes the request to one of the many instances of the blog server. However, note that even now we are using the same database for read and write operations.

Multi-availability zones

In the previous section, we talked about the single point of failure and why having multiple instances of the application server is a good thing. We can extend this concept further; what if we have all of our servers in one location and due to some major malfunction or outage, all of our servers go down? We will not be able to serve any user traffic.

We can see that having our servers in one location also creates a single point of failure. The solution for this would be to have application server instances available in multiple locations. Then the next question would be: how do we decide on the locations to deploy our servers? Should we deploy the servers to multiple locations within a single country or should we deploy them to multiple countries? We can rephrase the question using cloud computing terminology as follows.

We need to decide whether we want to deploy our servers to **multiple regions** or **multiple zones**, or perhaps a combination of both.

One important point to note is that deploying to multiple zones may lead to network delay and we may want to deploy to multiple regions first. However, before we deploy to multiple regions and zones, we need to make sure of two facts:

- Our website has heavy traffic that our single server setup is no longer able to handle
- We have a significant chunk of users from another country, and it might be a good idea to deploy servers in a zone near them

Once we have given consideration to these factors and decided to deploy to additional zones and regions, our blogging system as a whole might look something like this:

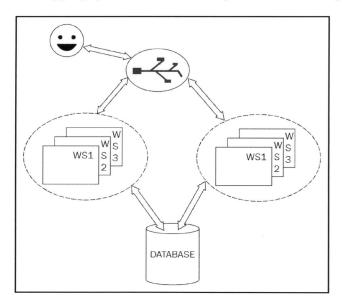

The database

We have been scaling the application/blog server and seen how to scale the server vertically and horizontally, and how to factor multiple zones and regions for high availability and performance of the overall system.

You may have noticed in all of the previous designs that we still relied on a single database instance. By now, you may have realized that having a single instance of any service/server can become a single point of failure and may bring the system to a complete standstill.

The tricky part is that we cannot use the straightforward strategy of running multiple database instances as we did for the application server. We were able to use this strategy for application server because the application server is responsible for business logic and what little state it maintains within itself is temporary, while all vital and important information is being pushed to the database which forms the single source of truth, and, ironically, the single source of failure. Before we dig deeper into the complexity of scaling a database and the challenges that come along with it, let us first look at an important topic that needs to be addressed.

SQL versus NoSQL

For the uninitiated, databases come in two varieties:

- **Relational databases**: These use SQL (with minor variations) for querying the database
- **NoSQL databases**: These can store unstructured data and use the database specific query language

Relational databases have been around for a long time now, and a lot of effort has been put into optimizing their performance and making them as robust as possible. However, the reliability and performance requires us to plan and organize our data into well-defined tables and relationships. Our data is bound to the schema of the database tables. Anytime we need to add more fields/columns to our table, we will have to migrate the table to a new schema, and this would require us to create migration scripts that take care of adding the new fields, and also to provide conditions and data to fill the newly created fields for the already existing rows in your table.

NoSQL databases tend to have a more free-form structure. We need not define schemas for our tables since data is stored as a single row/document. We can insert data of any schema into a single table and then query it. Given that the data is not confined to schema rules, we might end up inserting wrong or ill-formed data into our database. This means that we will have to deal with ensuring that we retrieve the correct data and also have to take precautions to ensure that data of different schemas do not crash the program.

Which type of database should we use?

At first, one might be tempted to go with NoSQL because then we don't need to worry about structuring our data and join queries. However, it is important to realize that, instead of writing these queries in SQL form, we will instead be retrieving all the data into the user space, that is, the program, and then write the manual join queries within the program.

Instead, if we rely upon relational databases, we can be assured of smaller storage space, more efficient join queries, and data with well-defined schemas. All relational databases and some of the NoSQL databases provide indexing, which also helps in optimizing for faster search queries. However, one major drawback of relational databases with using tables and joins is that, as the data grows bigger, it is possible that the joins will start getting slower. By this point, you will have a clear idea of which parts of your data can take advantage of NoSQL solutions, and you will start maintaining your data in a combination of SQL and NoSQL system.

In a nutshell, start with relational databases and, once you have a significant amount of data in your tables and no further database tuning can be done, then consider moving tables that really need the high performance of NoSQL datastores.

Database replication

Now that we have established why we are opting to use a relational database, let us move onto the next question: how can we ensure that our database doesn't become a single point of failure?

Let us first consider what are the consequences if a database fails:

- We cannot write new data to the database
- We cannot read from the database

Of the two consequences, the latter is more critical. Consider our blogging application, while being able to write new blog posts is important, the vast majority of the users on our site will be readers. This is the norm for most everyday user-facing applications. Hence, we should try to ensure that we are always able to read data from the database even if we are no longer able to write new data to it.

Database replication and redundancy try to address these issues and, generally, the solutions are included as part of the database or a plugin. In this section, we shall discuss three strategies used for database replication:

- Master-replica replication
- Master-master replication
- Failover cluster replication

Master-replica replication

This is the most straightforward method of replication. It can be explained as follows:

1. We take a cluster of databases:

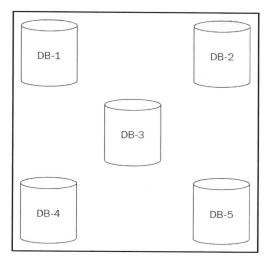

Cluster of databases

2. Designate one of them as the master, and the remaining databases as replicas:

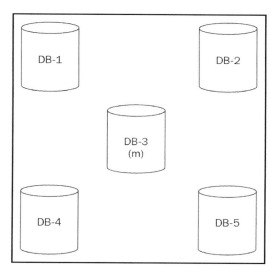

DB-3 is designated as the master

3. All writes are performed to the master:

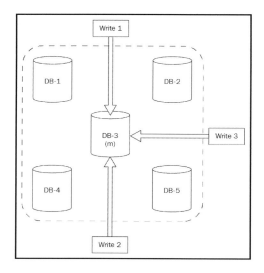

Three writes are performed on the master

4. All reads are performed from the replicas:

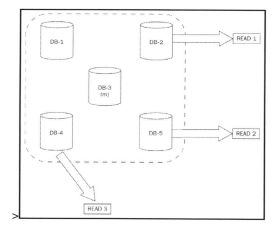

Reads performed from the replicas

5. The master ensures that all the replicas have the latest state which is the state of the master database:

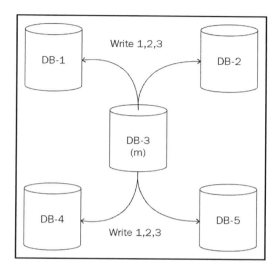

The master updates all the replicas with the latest update

6. Failure in master database still allows reads from replicant databases but writes are not possible:

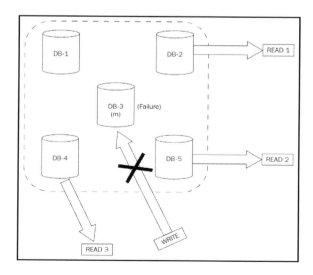

Master failure; no writes, only reads

Master-master replication

You may have noticed two issues with the master-replica setup:

- The master is used extensively for database writes, and hence is under constant duress
- The issue of reads has been solved with replicas but the single point of failure for writes is still present

Master-master replication tries to solve these issues by making every database a master. It can be explained as follows:

1. We take a cluster of databases:

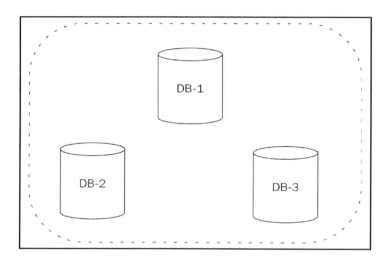

Cluster of databases

2. We designate every database as a master:

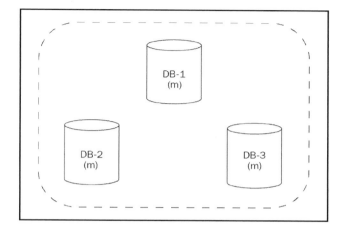

All databases are designated as a master

3. Reads can be performed from any of the masters:

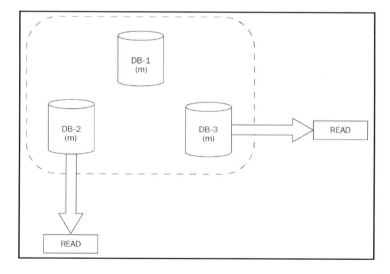

Reads performed on masters

4. Writes can be performed to any of the masters:

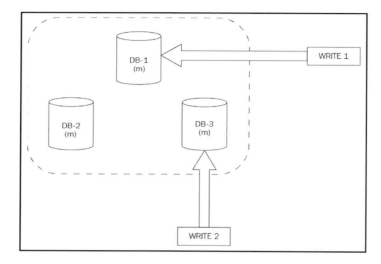

Writes made to DB-1 and DB-3

5. Every master updates every other master with the writes:

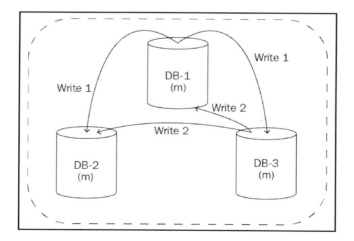

Database state synchronized across the masters

6. Hence, the state is maintained across all the databases:

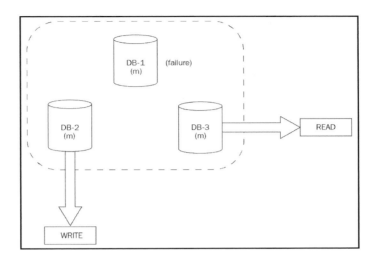

DB-1 failure, successful reads and writes

It may seem like this strategy works fine, but it has its own limitations and challenges; the major one being conflict resolution between writes. Here's a simple example.

We have two master-master databases **DB-1** and **DB-2**, and both have the latest state of the database system:

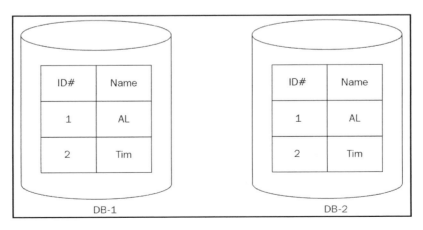

Latest state of DB-1 and DB-2

We have two simultaneous write operations to perform, so we send "Bob" to **DB-1** and "Alice" to **DB-2**.

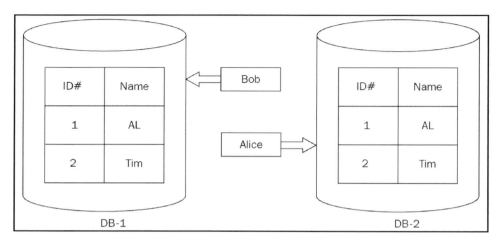

Write "Bob" to DB-1 and Write "Alice" to DB-2

Now that both databases have written the data to their tables, they need to update the other master with its own latest state:

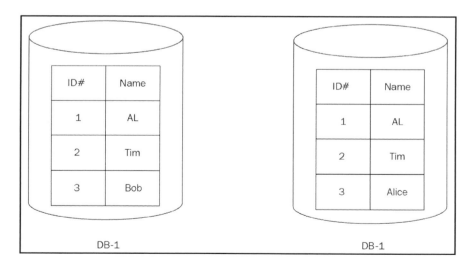

States before DB synchronization

This will lead to conflict because in both tables, **ID# 3** is populated with **Bob** for **DB-1** and **Alice** for **DB-2**:

Conflict while updating DB-1 and DB-2 states because ID# 3 is already populated.

In reality, the master-master strategy would have in-built mechanisms to deal with these kinds of issues, but they may induce a performance penalty or other challenges. This is a complex subject and we have to decide on what trade-offs are worth making if we want to use master-master replication.

Failover cluster replication

Master-replica replication allows us to have a simple setup for reads and writes at the potential risk of being unable to write to the master database. Master-master replication allows us to be able to read and write to the database even if one of the masters fail. However, the complexity of maintaining a consistent state across all the masters and the possible performance penalty can mean that it is not the ideal choice in all circumstances.

The failover cluster replication tries to take the middle ground by providing features of both replication strategies. It can be explained as follows:

1. We take a cluster of databases.
2. A database is assigned as the master depending on the master selection strategy used, which can vary from database to database.
3. The remaining databases are assigned as the replicas.

4. The master is responsible for updating the replicas with the latest state of the database.

5. If the master fails for some reason, a selection is made to assign one of the remaining databases as the new master.

So which replication strategy should we use? It would be best to start with the simplest one, that is, the master-replica strategy because this will cover most of initial needs with great ease. Let us now see what our application would look like if we used the master-replica strategy for database replication:

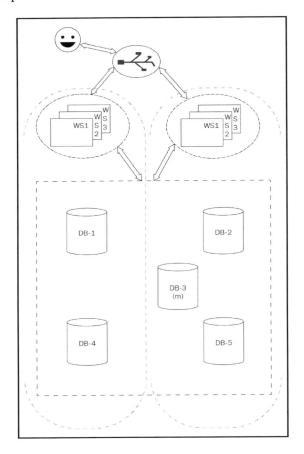

An application with the master-replica database setup

Monolith versus microservices

Most of the new projects start out as a single codebase where all the components interact with one another via direct function calls. However, as the user traffic and codebase increases, we will start facing issues with the codebase. Here are a few possible reasons for this:

- Your codebase is growing in size and this means that it will take longer for any new developer to understand the complete system.
- Adding a new feature will take longer because we have to make sure that the change doesn't break any of the other components.
- Redeploying code for every new feature might become cumbersome because of the following:
    - Deployment failed and/or
    - One of the redeployed components had an unexpected bug which crashed the program and/or
    - The build process may take longer because of a large number of tests
- Scaling the complete application to support a CPU intensive component

Microservices provide a solution to this by splitting up the major components of the application into separate smaller applications/services. Does this mean we should split our application from the start into microservices so that we don't face this issue? That is one possible way of approaching this subject. However, there are certain drawbacks to this approach as well:

- **Too many moving parts**: Dividing each component into its own service means that we will have to monitor and maintain servers for each of them.
- **Increased complexity**: Microservices increase the number of possible reasons for failure. Failures in a monolith may be limited to the server(s) going down or issues with code execution. However, with a microservice we have to:
    - Identify which component's server(s) went down or

- If a component fails, identify the failing component and then further investigate whether the failure was due to:
  - Faulty code or
  - Due to failure in one of the dependant components

- **Harder to debug the whole system**: The increased complexity described in the preceding points makes it harder to debug the complete system.

Now that we have seen some of the pros and cons of microservices and monolith architecture, which one is better? The answer should be fairly obvious by now:

- Small to medium-sized codebases benefit from the simplicity offered by a monolith
- Large codebases benefit from the granular control offered by the microservices architecture

This means that we should design our monolith codebase with the expectation that it might eventually grow to a very large size, and then we will have to refactor it into microservices. In order to make the task of refactoring the codebase into microservices as effortless as possible, we should identify the possible components as early as possible, and implement the interaction between them and the rest of the code using the **Mediator design pattern**.

Mediator design pattern

Mediator acts as an intermediary between components in the code, and this leads to very loose coupling between various components. This allows us to make minimal changes to the code, as we only need to change the interaction between the mediator and the component which is being extracted into its own microservice.

Let's look at an example. We have a monolith, which is defined by **Codebase A**. It consists of five components—**Component 1** through **Component 5**. We realize that **Component 1** and **Component 2** rely on interacting with **Component 5**, while **Component 2** and **Component 3** rely on **Component 4**. If **Component 1** and **Component 2** were to directly call **Component 5**, and similarly **Component 2** and **Component 4** were to directly call **Component 4**, then we would create tightly coupled components.

If we were to introduce a function that takes input from the calling components and calls the necessary component as a proxy, and if all data were passed using well-defined structs, then we would have introduced the mediator design pattern. This can be seen in the following figure:

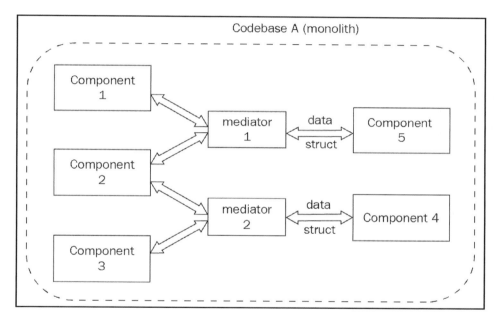

Components within a codebase connected via the mediator

Now if a situation arises where we might need to separate one of the components into its own separate microservices, we only need to change the implementation of the proxy function. In our example, `Component 5` is segregated into its own separate microservice, and we have changed the implementation of the proxy function **mediator 1** to communicate with **Component 5** using HTTP and JSON instead of communicating via function calls and structs. This is illustrated in the following figure:

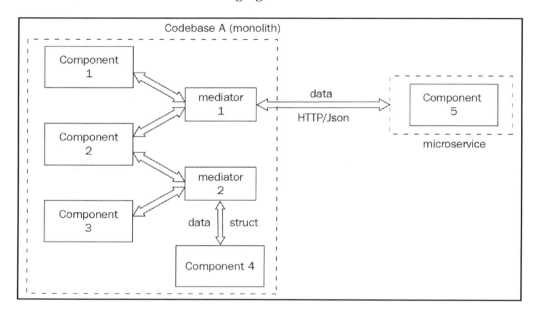

Component separated into a microservice and the change in the mediator implementation

Deployment options

We have looked at various strategies for scaling our application, different types of databases, how to structure our code, and finally how to use the mediator pattern to make the transition from monolith to microservices. However, we haven't discussed where we would be deploying said web application and databases. Let's take a brief look at the deployment landscape.

Till the early 2000s, most servers were deployed on hardware owned by the companies writing the software. There would be dedicated infrastructure and a team to deal with this critical part of software engineering. This was mostly the subject of data centers.

However, in the 2000s, companies began to realize that data centers could be abstracted away because most of the developers weren't interested in handling these problems. This allowed for cheaper and faster development and deployment of software, especially for web applications. Now, instead of buying hardware and space at a data center, the developers would be provided with server instances they could access via SSH. One of the most prominent companies in this field from the start was Amazon.com, Inc. This allowed them to expand their business beyond e-commerce.

These services also gave rise to the question: do developers need to install and maintain generic applications such as databases, load balancers, or other such services? The reality was that not all developers or companies wanted to be involved with maintaining these services. This created demand for ready-to-use application instances that would be maintained by the company selling these applications as a service.

There are many companies which initially started out as software companies that maintained their own data centers—Amazon, Google, and Microsoft to name a few examples—and they now boast a great set of such services for general consumption.

Maintainability of multiple instances

The availability of the mentioned services improve our life significantly yet there is a lot of complexity involved with maintaining a plethora of applications running across multiple server instances. For example:

- How can we update the server instances without bringing down the whole service? Can this be done with less effort?
- Is there a reliable way to scale our application (vertically and horizontally) with ease?

Given that all modern deployments make use of containers, we can make use of container orchestration software that helps with the maintainability issues. Kubernetes (https://kubernetes.io/) and Mesos (http://mesos.apache.org/) are examples of two such solutions.

Summary

In this chapter, we took the example of a simple blogging application and showed how we can scale it to meet the demands of growing user traffic. We also looked at the complexity and strategies involved with scaling databases.

We then took a brief look at how to architect our codebase and what the trade-offs are that we might need to consider. Finally, we looked at one approach to easily refactor our codebase from a monolith into microservices.

Other Books You May Enjoy

If you enjoyed this book, you may be interested in these other books by Packt:

Security with Go

John Daniel Leon

ISBN: 978-1-78862-791-7

- Learn the basic concepts and principles of secure programming
- Write secure Golang programs and applications
- Understand classic patterns of attack
- Write Golang scripts to defend against network-level attacks
- Learn how to use Golang security packages
- Apply and explore cryptographic methods and packages
- Learn the art of defending against brute force attacks
- Secure web and cloud applications

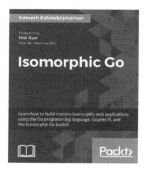

Isomorphic Go
Kamesh Balasubramanian

ISBN: 978-1-78839-418-5

- Create Go programs inside the web browser using GopherJS
- Render isomorphic templates on both the client side and the server side
- Perform end-to-end application routing for greater search engine discoverability and an enhanced user experience
- Implement isomorphic handoff to seamlessly transition state between the web server and the web browser
- Build real-time web application functionality with websockets
- Create reusable components (cogs) that are rendered using the virtual DOM
- Deploy an Isomorphic Go application for production use

Go Systems Programming

Mihalis Tsoukalos

ISBN: 978-1-78712-564-3

- Explore the Go language from the standpoint of a developer conversant with Unix, Linux, and so on
- Understand Goroutines, the lightweight threads used for systems and concurrent applications
- Learn how to translate Unix and Linux systems code in C to Golang code
- How to write fast and lightweight server code
- Dive into concurrency with Go
- Write low-level networking code

Leave a review - let other readers know what you think

Please share your thoughts on this book with others by leaving a review on the site that you bought it from. If you purchased the book from Amazon, please leave us an honest review on this book's Amazon page. This is vital so that other potential readers can see and use your unbiased opinion to make purchasing decisions, we can understand what our customers think about our products, and our authors can see your feedback on the title that they have worked with Packt to create. It will only take a few minutes of your time, but is valuable to other potential customers, our authors, and Packt. Thank you!

Index

Made in the USA
San Bernardino, CA
27 January 2019